What people are saying about

Resetting Our F⋯'

I

Our unequal world ha ⟨barcode T0154638⟩ asunder by a
pandemic and its econom⟨...⟩ ⟨...⟩es. In this bold book, Paul
O'Brien asks us to see how unfairly this crisis has landed, and to
confront the power and wealth inequalities at the heart of our
current economic system. It is an ambitious agenda, for sure, but
worth heeding if we want to emerge from this crisis with more
fairness, more humanity and more hope for the next generation.
Anne Kabagambe, Executive Director, The World Bank Group

The bad news is that the world is in crisis; the good news is
that transformative activism can overcome it; one key question
is whether the more formal progressive institutions – NGO,
foundations, think tanks and parties - will have the courage to
go all in with that activism, or whether they will keep trying
to hold on approval from a powerful establishment that is
breaking the world apart. Paul O'Brien knows all three of those
spaces – he's been a troublemaker, he's been a powerbroker,
and he's most recently spent a decade helping drive a leading
NGO. He sets out why we've got to where we are, and why now
is not a time for moderation. And whilst he warns us that we are
passing through a valley of death, he lets us know how we can
come through, and how we can take care of each other, and even
have fun together, while we do.
Ben Phillips is the author of *How to Fight Inequality* (Polity
Press). He is an advisor to the United Nations, governments and
civil society organizations, was Campaigns Director for Oxfam
Great Britain and for ActionAid, and co-founded the Fight
Inequality Alliance.

O'Brien understands the world as it is, not as international visionaries would like it to be, and from that solid base he sets out to correct ideological and structural problems. He traces the path of modern power relations right into the ideological framework of development programs like the Millennium and Sustainable Development Goals. Chillingly and convincingly, he warns that "if activists don't fight for the kind of power switch that protects the most vulnerable, even more power will be catastrophically redistributed away from those who need it most," pointing to evident power asymmetries in the spread and treatment of Covid-19, as auguries of a dark future. Though shaped by the realism of his experiences, this book, packed with precision, practical advice, and real-world experience, is richly seamed with hope for a better future, in which Covid-19 combines with humanism to create a better outlook for all.
Bernice Maxton-Lee, climate activist and author

Power Switch is a call to the activist in each of us. Our world will not be the same after this pandemic, nor will the global balance of power and money. If activists stay on the margins of economic decision making, we can only expect the powerful to get wealthier. If we work together, we can change the political equation for policy makers, and help to rebuild fair, just, and less wasteful economies. To find out precisely how, give this book a read. I, for one, am jumping in.
Stephanie Miller, Author of *Zero Waste Living, the 80/20 Way: The Busy Person's Guide to a Lighter Footprint* and Founder of Zero Waste in DC, and former Director, IFC Climate Business Department

RESETTING OUR FUTURE

Power Switch

How We Can Reverse Extreme Inequality

RESETTING OUR FUTURE

Power Switch

How We Can Reverse Extreme Inequality

Paul O'Brien

CHANGEMAKERS
BOOKS

Winchester, UK
Washington, USA

JOHN HUNT PUBLISHING

First published by Changemakers Books, 2021
Changemakers Books is an imprint of John Hunt Publishing Ltd., No. 3 East Street,
Alresford, Hampshire SO24 9EE, UK
office@jhpbooks.com
www.johnhuntpublishing.com
www.changemakers-books.com

For distributor details and how to order please visit the 'Ordering' section on our website.

Text copyright: Paul O'Brien 2020

ISBN: 978 1 78904 749 3
978 1 78904 750 9 (ebook)
Library of Congress Control Number: 2020947182

A CIP catalogue record for this book is available from the British Library.

Design: Stuart Davies

UK: Printed and bound by CPI Group (UK) Ltd, Croydon, CR0 4YY
Printed in North America by CPI GPS partners

We operate a distinctive and ethical publishing philosophy in
all areas of our business, from our global network of authors to
production and worldwide distribution.

Contents

The *Resetting Our Future* Series

At this critical moment of history, with a pandemic raging, we have the rare opportunity for a Great Reset – to choose a different future. This series provides a platform for pragmatic thought leaders to share their vision for change based on their deep expertise. For communities and nations struggling to cope with the crisis, these books will provide a burst of hope and energy to help us take the first difficult steps towards a better future.
– Tim Ward, publisher, Changemakers Books

What if Solving the Climate Crisis Is Simple?
Tom Bowman, President of Bowman Change, Inc., and Writing Team Lead for the U.S. ACE National Strategic Planning Framework

Zero Waste Living, the 80/20 Way
The Busy Person's Guide to a Lighter Footprint
Stephanie Miller, Founder of Zero Waste in DC, and former Director, IFC Climate Business Department.

A Chicken Can't Lay a Duck Egg
How COVID-19 can Solve the Climate Crisis
Graeme Maxton, (former Secretary-General of the Club of Rome), and Bernice Maxton-Lee (former Director, Jane Goodall Institute)

A Global Playbook for the Next Pandemic
Anne Kabagambe, World Bank Executive Director

Learning from Tomorrow
Using Strategic Foresight to Prepare for the Next Big Disruption
Bart Édes, North American Representative, Asian Development Bank

Impact ED
How Community College Entrepreneurship Programs Create Prosperity for All
Rebecca Corbin (President, National Association of Community College Entrepreneurship), Andrew Gold and Mary-Beth Kerly (both business faculty, Hillsborough Community College).

Power Switch
How We Can Reverse Extreme Inequality
Paul O'Brien, VP, Policy and Advocacy, Oxfam America

SMART Futures for a Sustainable World
Creating a Paradigm Shift for Achieving the Global SDGs
Dr. Claire Nelson, Chief Visionary Officer and Lead Futurist, The Futures Forum

Reconstructing Blackness
Rev. Charles Howard, Chaplin, University of Pennsylvania, Philadelphia.

Cut Super Climate Pollutants, Now!
The Ozone Treaty's Urgent Lessons for Speeding up Climate Action
Alan Miller (former World Bank representative for global climate negotiations) and Durwood Zaelke, (President, The Institute for Governance & Sustainable Development, and co-director, The Program on Governance for Sustainable Development at UC Santa Barbara)

www.ResettingOurFuture.com

"Pessimists are usually right and optimists are usually wrong but all the great changes have been accomplished by optimists."
Thomas Friedman

For Torin

Foreword

by Thomas Lovejoy

The Pandemic has changed our world. Lives have been lost. Livelihoods as well. Far too many face urgent problems of health and economic security, but almost all of us are reinventing our lives in one way or another. Meeting the immediate needs of the less fortunate is obviously a priority, and a big one. But beyond those compassionate imperatives, there is also tremendous opportunity for what some people are calling a "Great Reset." This series of books, *Resetting Our Future*, is designed to provide pragmatic visionary ideas and stimulate a fundamental rethink of the future of humanity, nature and the economy.

I find myself thinking about my parents, who had lived through the Second World War and the Great Depression, and am still impressed by the sense of frugality they had attained. When packages arrived in the mail, my father would save the paper and string; he did it so systematically I don't recall our ever having to buy string. Our diets were more careful: whether it could be afforded or not, beef was restricted to once a week. When aluminum foil – the great boon to the kitchen – appeared, we used and washed it repeatedly until it fell apart. Bottles, whether coca cola or milk, were recycled.

Waste was consciously avoided. My childhood task was to put out the trash; what goes out of my backdoor today is an unnecessary multiple of that. At least some of it now goes to recycling but a lot more should surely be possible.

There was also a widespread sense of service to a larger community. Military service was required of all. But there was also the Civilian Conservation Corps, which had provided jobs and repaired the ecological destruction that had generated the Dust Bowl. The Kennedy administration introduced the Peace

Corps and the President's phrase "Ask not what your country can do for you but what you can do for your country" still resonates in our minds.

There had been antecedents, but in the 1970s there was a global awakening about a growing environmental crisis. In 1972, The United Nations held its first conference on the environment at Stockholm. Most of the modern US institutions and laws about environment were established under moderate Republican administrations (Nixon and Ford). Environment was seen not just as appealing to "greenies" but also as a thoughtful conservative's issue. The largest meeting of Heads of State in history, the Earth Summit, took place in Rio de Janeiro in 1992 and three international conventions – climate change, biodiversity (on which I was consulted) and desertification – came into existence.

But three things changed. First, there now are three times as many people alive today as when I was born and each new person deserves a minimum quality of life. Second, the sense of frugality was succeeded by a growing appetite for affluence and an overall attitude of entitlement. And third, conservative political advisors found advantage in demonizing the environment as comity vanished from the political dialogue.

Insufficient progress has brought humanity and the environment to a crisis state. The CO_2 level in the atmosphere at 415 ppm (parts per million) is way beyond a non-disruptive level around 350 ppm. (The pre-industrial level was 280 ppm.)

Human impacts on nature and biodiversity are not just confined to climate change. Those impacts will not produce just a long slide of continuous degradation. The Pandemic is a direct result of intrusion upon, and destruction of, nature as well as wild-animal trade and markets. The scientific body of the UN Convention on Biological Diversity warned in 2020 that we could lose a million species unless there are major changes in human interactions with nature.

We still can turn those situations around. Ecosystem restoration at scale could pull carbon back out of the atmosphere for a soft landing at 1.5 degrees of warming (at 350 ppm), hand in hand with a rapid halt in production and use of fossil fuels. The Amazon tipping point where its hydrological cycle would fail to provide enough rain to maintain the forest in southern and eastern Amazonia can be solved with major reforestation. The oceans' biology is struggling with increasing acidity, warming and ubiquitous pollution with plastics: addressing climate change can lower the first two and efforts to remove plastics from our waste stream can improve the latter.

Indisputably, we need a major reset in our economies, what we produce, and what we consume. We exist on an amazing living planet, with a biological profusion that can provide humanity a cornucopia of benefits—and more that science has yet to reveal—and all of it is automatically recyclable because nature is very good at that. Scientists have determined that we can, in fact, feed all the people on the planet, and the couple billion more who may come, by a combination of selective improvements of productivity, eliminating food waste and altering our diets (which our doctors have been advising us to do anyway).

The *Resetting Our Future* series is intended to help people think about various ways of economic and social rebuilding that will support humanity for the long term. There is no single way to do this and there is plenty of room for creativity in the process, but nature with its capacity for recovery and for recycling can provide us with much inspiration, including ways beyond our current ability to imagine.

Ecosystems do recover from shocks, but the bigger the shock, the more complicated recovery can be. At the end of the Cretaceous period (66 million years ago) a gigantic meteor slammed into the Caribbean near the Yucatan and threw up so much dust and debris into the atmosphere that much of biodiversity perished. It was *sayonara* for the dinosaurs; their only surviving close relatives were precursors to modern day birds. It certainly was not a good time for life on Earth.

The clear lesson of the pandemic is that it makes no sense to generate a global crisis and then hope for a miracle. We are lucky to have the pandemic help us reset our relation to the Living Planet as a whole. We already have building blocks like the United Nations Sustainable Development Goals and various environmental Conventions to help us think through more effective goals and targets. The imperative is to rebuild with humility and imagination, while always conscious of the health of the living planet on which we have the joy and privilege to exist.

Dr. Thomas E. Lovejoy is Professor of Environmental Science and Policy at George Mason University and a Senior Fellow at the United Nations Foundation. A world-renowned conservation biologist, Dr. Lovejoy introduced the term "biological diversity" to the scientific community.

Acknowledging Some Facts & Folks

This book took me three decades. I wrote most of it in Western Ireland over the summer of 2020, but the ideas in here have been percolating for most of my life as an activist.

A bit of background: I emigrated to the U.S. in the early 1980s at the beginning of the Reagan years, and came to love this crazy country for its possibilities, even as I saw its President declare war on his own government. Landing as an Irish migrant with no money and no work visa in New Orleans, I ended up owning a small restaurant on Bourbon Street and saved enough money to finish college. Only in America would Harvard Law School like that story and lend me all the money I needed to get a *Juris Doctorate*.

With a fancy degree in hand, I chased my life partner to Nairobi, and with some amazing Kenyan friends, began to organize activists in Nairobi's slums during their first multiparty elections. I was, and still am, a zealous convert to America's offer to the world: "government of the people, by the people, for the people."

After a sojourn back in the U.S. where I worked in a big New York law firm, ran a social justice foundation, and repaid my school loans, I headed back to live in Uganda, Pakistan, Afghanistan and eventually Kenya again, trying to become an effective international activist. My most life-altering experience in that period was in Afghanistan, when after years as an advocate for CARE U.S. calling on the U.S. government and Afghan leaders to change their approach to rebuilding that country, the U.S. paid for me to become the advisor to Ashraf Ghani, now the President of Afghanistan, to help put his ideas into practice. His ideas on state building and the role that the U.S. should play in the world changed my own world view as an activist, and profoundly shaped the arguments I make in this book.

In 2007, I returned to the U.S. and since then have had the privilege of leading Oxfam America's advocacy work. For most of 2020, I was seconded to Oxfam International to co-lead Oxfam's advocacy response to the COVID-19 pandemic. Oxfam is a worldwide network that works with partners to fight inequality to beat poverty. It has no political affiliation in any country and is non-partisan.

In April of 2021, I will take a long-planned professional break to relocate to Connemara. As this part of my professional life draws to a close, I feel so grateful for having worked at Oxfam and for the friends I've made there. I can think of no better place to work with activists across borders to fight for social justice. Writing this book has allowed me to reflect on my work at Oxfam, and author something personal, with my own views about power, politics, today's injustices and tomorrow's possibilities. To the extent the ideas in this book differ from Oxfam's published work, they are my own personal views. This book has not been reviewed or endorsed by Oxfam in any way. Where I draw from Oxfam's published work, I cite the sources in endnotes and the bibliography.

With that said, I need to acknowledge the influence of Oxfam colleagues over my thinking. First, I am grateful to Ray Offenheiser, Oxfam America's former President and CEO who hired me into my current role, and my current boss, Oxfam America President and CEO, Abby Maxman, who generously supported my secondment to co-lead Oxfam's international influencing effort during COVID-19. My co-leader in this effort was Lan Mercado, who was based in Manila, twelve hours ahead of Washington D.C., and we "followed the sun" over many early morning and late evening chats. In this global effort, both of us reported to the ever graceful, smart and patient Steve Price Thomas, Oxfam's Policy Director. Steve gave us wise counsel, guidance and oversight in this worldwide influencing effort and helped to shape or refine many of the policies Oxfam now calls for publicly.

At the core of the advocacy efforts throughout the pandemic was a "coordination group" of thinkers, writers and activists from around the world who helped steer the Oxfam advocacy ship, and I borrowed from their ideas and energy at will in writing this book including: Nabil Ahmed, Charlotte Becker, Kala Constantino, Mamata Dash, Raina Fox, Matt Grainger, Victoria Harnett, Max Lawson, Lan Mercado, Ed Pomfret, Anna Ratcliff, Julie Thekkudan, Mat Truscott, Manal Warde, and Deepak Xavier.

For more than three decades I've been strategizing on how to redistribute power with fellow activists and need to acknowledge a few who shaped the ideas in this book: Tariq Ahmed, Reyn Anderson, Nazanin Ash, Jaime Atienza, Judy Beals, Phil Bloomer, Niall Brennan, Tosca Bruno-van Vijfeijken, Winnie Byanyima, Lindsay Coates, Nathan Coplin, Gina Cummings, Nadia Daar, Barbara Durr, Adib Farhadi, Tom Hart, Didier Jacobs, Nick Galasso, Ian Gary, Paulina Garzon, Mburu Gitu, Kent Glenzer, Duncan Green, Becks Gowland, Ben Grossman-Cohen, Gawain Kripke, Matt Harrington, George Ingram, Chris Jochnick, Michael Klosson, Nancy Lindborg, Clare Lockhart, Lora Lumpe, Katya Maia, Ton Meijers, Muthoni Muriu, Nora O'Connell, Bill O'Keefe, Scott Paul, Andrea Perera, Kimberly Pfeiffer, Ben Phillips, Dafna Rand, David Ray, Rebecca Rewald, Stephen Rickard, Bernice Romero, Sonal Shah, Smita Singh, Sarah Tuckey, Matthew Spencer, Danny Sriskandarajah, Dawn Stallard, Alex Thier, Noam Unger, Alexey Volynets, Iona Volynets, Andrew Wilder and Bob Zachritz. I feel very lucky to have debated how to redistribute power and tackle inequality with all these people, but any mistakes in here are solely mine.

Because the books in this series aim to be contemporary, I wrote and edited it at speed. I could never have done that without the wisdom and editorial genius of Tim Ward who asked me to take on this project, and the editing and encouragement of my great friend Stephanie Miller who wrote her inspiring book, *Zero Waste Living, the 80/20 Way* (forthcoming, John Hunt Publishing), during the same time frame (and just a bit faster than me). Thanks to Raquel Gomes, for her incisive editing and constant support when this endeavor felt impossible. Most of all I want to thank my life partner, Kath Campbell, who I fell in love with 28 years ago, not just because she was the best editor I'd ever met, but because she laughed at my jokes—I'm so lucky that she still is and does. Finally, as the parent of an emerging activist who just left for college in these strange times, I often asked myself "would Torin read this" as I wrote. Thanks for your inspiration Torin. This book is for you.

Prologue: A Possible Future

Imagine this: The pandemic is finally in remission. A "people's vaccine" has been manufactured and distributed free of charge in every country in the world, reaching the world's largest slums in Nairobi, Mumbai, Mexico City, Cape Town and Karachi. Even as millions still wait for the vaccine, most believe they can fight off hunger and recover their health as lockdowns are lifted.

Many people don't remember who initially produced this life-saving vaccine. World leaders demanded that it be patent-free and go first to those who could not survive economically or physically through social distancing, hand washing, and mask wearing. The fears of vaccine nationalism—rich northern countries hoarding and awash in vaccines while the most vulnerable died—disappeared with the fading memories of populist despots who lost power in 2020.

People are breathing. In the U.S., they breathe with less fear of police violence or racial or sexual abuse. While some conservative American commentators rant on about the loss of U.S. primacy and leadership in 2021, most Americans like what's happened to its global role. A reenergized U.S. Government is offering partnership, not leadership, to the world. As it no longer claims "indispensability" or "exceptionalism," the U.S. has become more useful to tackling global challenges, joining an interstate partnership of like-minded allies broader than the UN Security Council, G7 or G20 to confront the extreme inequalities of wealth and power that are leaving people behind in China and Chattanooga, Nairobi and New York.

A renewed faith in government ripples across the globe. Middle-income and rich nations are replenishing their national budgets with progressive taxes where the wealthy and corporations pay a greater share than they have in four decades. Stimulus packages and social floors have helped the most vulnerable to navigate economic hardships, and unemployment numbers are dropping.

As economies awaken, a new generation of stateswomen and men are working together more than they have in years to build a "human economy" with fairness and health for all at its core. They have embraced policies that reduce carbon extraction and further nurture the planet and its people. The food that is returning to market shelves is healthier, informal workers have better protections, the sick can rely on better public health care. "Virtual education," once an oxymoron, is now a real choice for youth even in remote parts of countries.

So-called "fragile" and lower income countries from Afghanistan to Zimbabwe, are spending precious savings from debt relief and newly allocated global reserves to stabilize communities, provide some cash payments to those who can't yet find work, and strengthen their public health systems. As the pandemic raged throughout 2020, more people died from hunger than from the virus itself. Now, hunger related deaths are dropping drastically.

A transformed American political landscape was one of the catalysts for this transformation. In 2021, the Biden and Harris Administration went beyond simply restoring the dynamics and institutions of the past. To win the 2020 election, they ran on the most progressive domestic and international agenda of any Democratic ticket in four decades. Knowing that moderate voters would show up to end the madness of the Trump years, they focused on energizing the working poor, youth and people of color in their base constituencies and in swing states. They offered the promise of a new social contract for all Americans. To be an American, they reminded us, is not just to be guaranteed civil and political rights, but economic and social protection, basic employment rights and a fair playing field in working toward one's dreams.

American progressives agreed. They connected the national

political moment with the international fight against inequality. They knew that as the pandemic receded, there would be a window for leaders to come together on global climate commitments, to end tax havens, to cancel poor country debts and to launch the kinds of new funding mechanisms that would redistribute power and wealth to vulnerable communities. They joined with domestic activists in the U.S. fighting for labor rights, racial and gender justice, reproductive and voting rights. Together, they called out, stalled and began to reverse the inequalities of power that four decades of neoliberal, trickle-down governance and economics had reaped on the U.S. and the world.

The Purpose and Structure of this Book

Sound farfetched? Too optimistic for this moment in history? This book aims to convince you that such a massive power switch is possible and could begin in the next couple of years. This pandemic could be the catalyst for a massive transformation of power relations, a new social contract in the U.S., and a shared global struggle between activists around the world to confront and defeat an "inequality virus"[1] that left us unprepared for this pandemic and its economic consequences.

Young and progressive activists have been feeling our planet's temperature rising, literally and figuratively. If the rest of us are proverbial frogs in a rapidly warming pot, unable before this pandemic to marshal the collective political will to protect our economy, planet or ourselves, COVID-19 has lifted us from our increasingly tepid home and plonked us into a near boiling cauldron. This book claims that young activists, witnessing this change, and far more concerned about its long-term consequences, are demanding we do something. If we listen to them, we can help them turn on a power switch that reshapes our world.

The book has two parts. Part One describes how international activism is in a moment of crisis and explores the opportunity for transformative change. Chapter 1 defines "international activist" and surfaces three dilemmas with which American activists need to reckon to stay relevant. Chapter 2 proposes that we will need to get more fluent in the language of "power" and debates on power redistribution to be relevant to a global power switch. And Chapter 3 argues that in this unique moment, power will be distributed for better or worse.

Part Two focuses on extreme economic inequality as an area where a power switch is both necessary and possible. Chapter 4 lays out the power inequality crisis and opportunity we will face after this pandemic. Chapter 5 suggests specific strategies that activists should consider if they want to be part of a global power switch that reduces inequality, and Chapter 6 proposes specific policy reforms on which activists should focus. In my conclusion, I suggest some actions you, as readers, could take.

If this book works for you the way I hope it will, it will leave you thinking differently about power and international activism, and hopefully provoke you to unleash your inequality activist.

Part One

Activism Crisis as Opportunity

Chapter 1

International Activism: A Field in Flux

The world has been cursed by people who tailored themselves as international visionaries. Every global war since the Crusades, colonialism, slavery, and the expansion of religious ideology and the sectarian violence that has often followed, were led by "visionaries" who saw the world beyond their national borders and wanted to impact it in the name of some greater good. Not one of them claimed that their purpose was ruinous, but damage they did, destroying millions of lives and plundering the planet's resources.

What makes today's international activists different from histories' megalomaniacs? How do we know whether international activism will make life better for others? This chapter aims to answer the first question. The remainder of the book aims to answer the second.

I think of "international activists" as those people and institutions with three characteristics:

Their power is private but their interest is public.,

They seek to change our world for the better by redistributing *power*, not just resources.

They seek changes that are explicitly and intentionally beyond their own national borders.

International activism is now grappling with a dilemma in each of these spaces.

Who are Activists? Private Power and Public Purpose

To be an activist means two things: Your power comes from a certain place and your purpose is to achieve a particular outcome. Consider the following table which differentiates activists from politicians and people in the for-profit world.

Power			
		Public	**Private**
Purpose	**Public**	The state and interstate actors	Activists
	Private	State actors who use public power for private gain	The private sector

The state and interstate actors: Here are the elected officials, state employees, governments and intergovernmental bodies that have mandated power to shape our world. In a health and economic pandemic, political leaders from New Zealand's Jacinda Arden to Donald Trump in the U.S., from local mayors to the UN Secretary General seek international outcomes to advance their official interests. They have to. That's the reality a pandemic forces on them. They are state actors with publicly mandated power whose purpose—officially—is to advance the interests of their citizens, and they know in a pandemic, the solutions they need often lie beyond their borders. They are active internationally, but for our purposes in this book, they are not "international activists." They are, however, the main target that activists seek to influence.

The private sector: Much to the frustration of activists, the private sector constantly prioritizes profit making for owners over other values. With consumers becoming more active, employees demanding a mission to believe in, and governments waking up to corporate power, some corporate leaders are evolving, but not fast enough. From tech billionaires who have watched their profits soar in this pandemic to the private hospital executives trying to source protective gear, the private sector is also active internationally, but their purpose at the end of the day is still overly driven by their bottom lines. No one voted for Zuckerberg and Bezos to change the world, even as they have gained more power to do so than most state actors. For that reason, they are often the rightful target of international activism.

Activists: This book is written for and about activists, individuals who have no public authority, but who claim a public purpose: to make our world better.

Some of those activists work professionally in social justice organizations and international non-governmental organizations (INGOs), like Oxfam. The public may support us by contributing their voice, actions and money to our causes, but they didn't vote for us. These organizations no longer sit exclusively in Europe and the U.S., but all over the world. Even the globally networked organizations with deep roots in the North, increasingly have their headquarters in the South. Oxfam is run out of Nairobi, Action Aid out of Johannesburg, and BRAC, the world's largest INGO, is headquartered in Dhaka, Bangladesh. That's not to say we are all now globally balanced networks and seen as legitimate players in the countries where we work—far from it. But some INGOs are less accurately today described as "Northern charities" that bestow largess on an unsuspecting world with little reflection about their roots or legitimacy.

Not all professional international activists work for INGOs. Once they became global philanthropists, Bill Gates and Lorena Powell Jobs joined our ranks and brought along many others in their organizations. Individual influencers like Malala Yousafzai, Greta Thunberg, Naomi Klein, Anand Giridharadas, and Nick Kristoff are international activists: their power is private, and their stated purpose is public.

You don't have to be paid or famous to be an activist. If you are reading this because you care about power and wealth inequality in our world and want to do something about it by reshaping how governments and corporations act, then you are an activist, and you are indispensable to any power switch that may happen after this pandemic.

As I argue in Part Two of this book, establishment politicians and corporate leaders will not advance a transformation of power and wealth in our world unless they believe that it is what voters and consumers need, expect and demand from them. Effective activists change what power brokers decide, by transforming the imagination and energies of those around them, provoking new debates and changing beliefs in what is possible in politics and business. When we do this, we exercise a form of power that can redistribute control over resources from those who have too much to those on the wrong end of inequality.

What makes us "Activists" rather than just Actors

Every sector has its tropes, the shallow truisms and certainties into which we strand ourselves. Two of the more toxic tropes in the INGO "development sector" are that our purpose is to "teach people to fish, not feed them" and ultimately "work ourselves out of a job." We declare these things in the hope that our impact will be lasting, and to humbly acknowledge that feeding someone for a day relegates power to the giver, generating dependency in the process.

Those tropes dominate our sector. You won't find a government donor or large INGO who claims "we just treat symptoms and do nothing really to help people help themselves."[1] Nor are we likely to admit "we plan to stay here as long as there are unnecessary inequalities of power and resources that will make life unfair or unsustainable." Everyone is always promising to leave soon, job done. We fool ourselves and few others.

It's the trope *itself* that is the problem. They are not just banal but harmless marketing slogans. The reason people are not "fishing" (farming, trading, building) through this pandemic, is less because no one showed them how to fish before this moment, and more because fishing is (and may have always been) impossible for them. Before the pandemic, it might have been because a factory upstream polluted the water, a public dam that drained the fish-filled rivers, the local landowner who blocked their access to the waters, or a buyer that extorted an unfair price. In this pandemic, it might be because of lockdowns (you may not fish), the disruption of supply chains (there are no hooks to buy nor markets to sell your wares), or because hunger is robbing the most destitute of the energy and health to help themselves.

Right now, vulnerable people in the U.S. and around the world need two things: Some just need to be given fish to stay alive, and they need the powerful actors around them—the private sector and public bodies—to create the conditions in which they can go back to protecting their livelihoods. They don't need a lesson in casting.

Humanitarian and charitable individuals and organizations all over the world right now are giving people "fish" and saving lives by doing so. Organizations like Oxfam are transferring cash and in-kind support—sometimes food—to hundreds of thousands of people to help them get a meal a day and survive through this pandemic. The United Nations is coordinating multi-billion-dollar efforts to try and stop 12,000 people a day dying from hunger (more people than are dying from the virus itself). That's essential life-saving work.

At the same time, international *activists* are challenging the powerful to do more to help and less to harm those who are already vulnerable. Particularly in this moment where the rules of life and living are shifting dramatically, we need international activists to *influence* change by others and not exclusively seek to deliver the change ourselves.

The reason people aren't fishing their way through this pandemic and most of the other inequalities and shocks they face is not because "they" need to be changed, but because those with economic or political power around them—the super wealthy, governments, corporations and international bodies—are failing to create a world in which vulnerable people can feed themselves.

Activists Beyond Borders

Lastly, to be an international activist means believing something about *where* your activism aims to deliver impact. Most activists work in and on their own local communities. For some, seeking national-level policy and practice change is how they express their patriotism, their franchise as nationals, and how they strengthen the social contract as citizens with their state.

International activism is about changing power relationships and asymmetries outside of your own country: whether you write a post to witness the torture of a political prisoner in an oppressive regime or join a global movement to impact the rules, rights and resources that govern humankind. We seek change beyond borders. We see a shared humanity, a vision for better lives everywhere.

For the international activist who wants to work on the systemic drivers of extreme economic inequality, our aim is often to foment national level policy change in other countries or shift the policies of global economic powers like the U.S. or China, corporations like Amazon or Exxon, or multilateral institutions like the International Monetary Fund or United Nations.

Emerging Challenges for International Activism

The three characteristics that define us each raises its own question that is fundamentally shifting how we work.

A question of legitimacy. If we claim a public purpose but have no public mandate and no legal authority, if no one voted for us and therefore we have no right to represent anyone, what legitimate authority do international activists have to change power dynamics?

The political nature of power. If we are not just helping people, giving them fish or teaching them how to fish—charitable and technical challenges—but challenging the systems in which they may or may not fish in the first place, then we are engaging in a form of political action (if politics is a power struggle over rules, institutions, resources, values and mindsets). Not all our supporters expect or want us to become political actors. The leaders and elites that we challenge around the world rarely do. They allow international purpose-driven organizations and individuals to work in their countries if they are there to help, to fill gaps in social services, to transfer resources and skills, but they rarely want "guests" to challenge their power, hold them accountable, and often name and shame them in the process.

Social contracts are usually local not global. Finally, if purpose-driven activism does have a natural legitimacy in this world, isn't it closer to home, as part of a social contract: when one pays taxes, votes, serves in and benefits from public institutions and services, one has a right to a political voice? What gives activists the right to distribute power across borders?

These questions have always weighed on international activists, but in the last decade more so. Increasingly, for example, activists in the global south and north are *not* okay with international organizations or global activism being run by well-meaning northerners who claim not just a public purpose to help people overseas but a sometimes unexamined authority to do so. It is worth taking a moment to look at some of the roots of international anti-poverty activism.

Activist History & Its Baggage

The tone, tactics and strategies for most coordinated global activism on poverty over the past four decades has often been fomented, and often led, by English, Irish, and to a lesser extent,

American activists—many of them white men. Celebrity activists like Band Aid's Bob Geldof and Bono, who founded ONE, created a massive amount of public energy to address global poverty crises in the 1980s and 1990s. The battle against debt which Oxfam helped to start in the 1980s, in the UK,[2] advocated that "for every £1 we all give for famine relief in Africa in 1985, the West took back £2 in debt payments."2 By 2000, the global debt movement was, in the eyes of one commentator, David Roodman, "very much driven by a British invasion. Oxfam's early pressure turned the UK government into the strongest advocate for debt relief among the Group of Seven leading industrial nations."[3] Oxfam, a member of Jubilee 2000, hosted a meeting in Washington which led to the founding of the Center on Global Development to make the ongoing case for debt relief.[4] The combination of deep and politically powerful research, and inclusive movement building that brought together uncommon groups delivered a huge redistribution of wealth during the Jubilee campaign.

Oxfam and other British activists also launched the *Make Poverty History* campaign in 2005 and the *Enough Food for Everyone IF* campaign in 2013.[5] Those campaigns and the growth of foreign aid levels were not without their critiques. Southern intellectuals like Dambisa Moyo (author of *Dead Aid*, 2009), Northerners like Bill Easterly (*The White Man's Burden: Why the West's Efforts to Aid the Rest have Done So Much Ill and So Little Good*, 2007), and more contemporary critics calling for aid that is less colonial, more anti-racist,[6] and more feminist,[7] all share a common tenet: the international development sector has fallen short of redistributing resources and power to its intended beneficiaries.

That failure is increasingly obvious to the new generation of young activists in international organizations and their partners in the South. If foreign aid is going to redistribute power, they argue, then it needs to be thought of and delivered in an entirely new way, starting with a re-envisioning of international organizations, how they are staffed, from which sources they get their money, and how they organize themselves in governance structures. These are some of the questions that Tosca Bruno-van Vijfeiken and her co-authors grapple with in *Between Power and Irrelevance: The Future of Transnational NGOs*, (2020), and to which I return in my conclusion.

Chapter 2

A Strange Thing about Power and Money

So international activism is about redistributing power from the haves to the have nots across the globe. To make that case, I need to unpack what I mean by "power," and how we redistribute it, and then turn to the relationship between redistributing power and redistributing wealth.

Two Ways to Get Power

The word power has two core meanings in English and some other languages: one is an ability (I feel "powerful" today), and the other is a relationship (when you exercise power over me). Most of us use both meanings interchangeably and know what we mean.

"I felt so empowered by that book" (that is power as ability).

"I don't have the power to make you clean your room" (power as a lack of control).

"I could feel the people power at that protest" (ability again).

"Marches don't matter until we take power away from narcissistic autocrats" (a desire for control).

For more than 400 years, influential thinkers debated the importance, exercise and typologies of power, but they essentially agreed on one thing: power was about control, and it was a like a currency—if power was held by some, it could not be held by others. A largely male, largely northern cast of thinkers explained the world in this way. Thomas Hobbes brought us "state power," embodied by *Leviathan's* dominance of unruly masses (Hobbes, 1651). Similarly, Max Weber believed that state power consisted in a "monopoly of the legitimate use of physical force" (Weber, 1919). Friedrich Nietzsche took the debate beyond the state to include "the will to power" that each individual can exercise *over* others. In the influential *Power: A Radical View,* (Lukes, 1974) Stephen Lukes carried on the tradition of framing power as a struggle for control. All these men essentially conceived of power as a zero-sum currency — essentially *the ability to control or influence the resources, actions and even innermost thoughts of oneself or others.* They debated who had power, who should have it, and how to distribute it, but they took for granted that power is a currency that, if held by some, cannot not be owned by others.

Then, along came Foucault (1926–1984). Together with other post-modernists, Foucault sought new ways of thinking about language, ideas, identity and ourselves. Foucault had watched the philosophers of language of his time (including his own *Words and Things*) lose relevance and energy in the search for grand unifying ideas to explain everything by limiting our thinking to "their" lens on life. He witnessed in *Discipline and Punish* and *The History of Sexuality* how the oppression of nations, prisoners, colonized peoples and even our bodies, can be better understood by opening up our thinking to different theories, types and definitions of power realized in action.[1]

Of course, it wasn't just Foucault who helped to shape modern thinking about power. Post-modernism didn't just reveal the northern white male heterosexual hegemony over intellectual life. For the last thirty years, the identities and voices that are shaping the power debate has changed. Feminists from both the North[2] and South,[3] advocates for racial justice,[4] class justice,[5] sexual and reproductive rights,[6] movement builders,[7] and those insisting on a better global balance of voices that are heard have transformed our understanding of power.

By the late twentieth century those activists had had enough of the zero-sum power frame. They rejected the language of the privileged and embraced power as "ability." "Empowerment" became central to social change and activism, and by empowerment, people mostly meant power as ability —

it was a form of power that could be grown without conflict, without zero-sum choices that usually went the wrong way.[8] Feminist thinkers and Southern activists in particular exposed how zero-sum power relationships had been exercised largely by "hegemonic masculinity" to subjugate others throughout history. They wanted a definition of power that was less zero-sum and more generative. To the extent they saw power as a relationship, they were more interested in how a person might stimulate, support and lift the power of themselves or others, rather than control or dominate others in a zero-sum game. That choice—to think more about power as an ability that could be grown in oneself or others without anyone losing—had plenty of merits, but it also came with a cost that weakened the effectiveness of international activism.

Why is this debate about "power" important for international activists?

Until the mid-1980s, modern international activism had a singular tone: anti-apartheid, anti-racism, anti-nuke; the fight against the AIDS pandemic, for Central America solidarity; the drive for human rights and challenging power elites in South Africa, China, the U.S. and other places.[9] They were angry movements meant to redistribute power meant as "control"— employing boycotts, divestment, civil disobedience, naming and shaming. "We're watching you," they said to elites. "Meet our demands or else."

And then, something changed. International development thinkers, third wave feminists, and other justice advocates reframed the conversation about power (I analyze that reframing in a chapter of a book).[10] Essentially, international activism ended up with an understanding of "Empowerment" that wasn't redistributive or zero-sum. It was generative and win-win. "I am powerful," the posters claimed, with the speaker empowered as a rights bearer, front and center. There

26

was never a duty bearer in those posters—the powerful actor against whom her rights might be asserted. The humanitarian vision saw no need for losers or the ugliness of conflict.

If we were going to wipe out extreme poverty, international activists decided, we needed positive not negative energy. More pragmatically, we needed to make sure not to make enemies of the very individuals and institutions whose power we were challenging if our vision was to be realized. And so, we rejected zero-sum thinking as unconstructive and unlikely to yield the results we wanted.

It wasn't just smart campaigning. It was an operational necessity for international organizations whose primary mission and main fundraising story was to distribute life-saving resources in crises. Reaching vulnerable communities often required the permission of warring parties and corrupt autocrats. Naming and shaming them was impossible if we wanted to fulfill our humanitarian missions.

And so, we jumped on the *Band-Aid* wagon in the 1980s, embraced *Make Poverty History* in the 1990s, celebrated first the Millennium Development Goals in 2000, and then the Sustainable Development Goals in 2015. In campaign after campaign international activists fought to mobilize and empower the world against... no one.

When I went from being a human rights campaigner to a development activist in the 1990s, I became part of that "empowerment" world. It allowed me to live in places and meet with people that I could never have reached as a human rights warrior. I would never have been allowed to document the costs of the Sudanese government's oppressive policies in the Nuba Mountains. I would never have interviewed SPLM leader John Garang in Nairobi, Abdul Haq in Kabul or Paul Wolfowitz in Washington. I would not have gotten to work with women activists in Afghanistan during the Taliban years or work with Ashraf Ghani in post-9/11 Afghanistan. My passport to these experiences was the win-win offer of development activism. We offered power for the oppressed without taking it from the oppressors. I didn't understand it that way at the time and am not apologizing for it now, but I have come to believe that win-win activism has its unseen costs.

The cost of ignoring power redistribution

A management guru once told me "the problem for many executives is not their weaknesses, but the overuse of strengths." The exclusive focus on power as ability was too much of a good thing and left us unprepared for the extreme asymmetries of political, economic and social power that are now wreaking havoc in this pandemic.

When international activism frames everything as a "win-win," it overuses a strength. If we are to be a relevant force in the economic reset that is to come, we must balance out our thinking about power as ability, with a more honest and relevant activism that names power as control.

Why make this distinction now? Particularly during and after this pandemic, shouldn't development activists keep looking for win-wins to crowd in more positive energy, more resources, and more political will to address the health, economic and social aftershocks of this pandemic around the world? If we want to provide an alternative to populist demagoguery, why embrace zero-sum thinking? After a period of economic contraction, shouldn't we just be getting back to work, back to growth, and worry about how the pie gets split later? If everyone has enough to eat again, what does it matter that a few billionaires increased their fortunes many-fold in this pandemic, just as they have in the past decade (see Chapter Four for the scale of their wealth)? What harm is there in the super wealthy having a few more toys and a little more power?

The rest of this book lays out the answer in facts and analysis: we have reached a level of inequality in this pandemic that a power switch — a massive redistribution of wealth and power — is inevitable. The problem is that it can swing either way. If activists don't fight for the kind of power switch that protects the most vulnerable, even more power will be catastrophically redistributed *away* from those who need it most.

Power and Wealth Debates Share the Same Question

Economic policy usually ends up focusing on a similar question: Do we grow the pie or split it differently? Do we create more wealth in the world or redistribute what we have? In the last forty years, the global economy has grown from less than $20 trillion to more than $85 trillion,[11] and growing the pie has become the obsession of economic policy-making while sharing the pie more fairly has largely been ignored. "For good reason," growth advocates argued: growth is the lifeblood of capitalism, makes conflict resolution easier, and if the pie is divided fairly to begin with, it provides more for everyone.

Today, more people are realizing that growth extremism depends on flawed assumptions: that it can be achieved without exhausting our natural resources and crashing through planetary boundaries necessary for our health and well-being; that on its own, it can bring us together, resolve conflicts and improve life for everyone equitably; and that the power that comes with more wealth for some will be managed in a way that leaves everyone better off.

As I lay out in Part Two, growth extremism is making our world toxically unequal in terms of both wealth and power. Activists want a different kind of economics and politics. In the U.S. and across the world, bolstered by the unequal impact of the pandemic, we are seeing a resurgence of redistributive politics, and sustainable economics to better control the power and wealth of those who have too much.

Chapter 3

When Power Switches Happen

Milton Friedman, the neoliberal economist once wrote:

Only a crisis—actual or perceived—produces real change. When that crisis occurs, the actions that are taken depend on the ideas that are lying around. That, I believe, is our basic function: to develop alternatives to existing policies, to keep them alive and available until the politically impossible becomes politically inevitable.[1]

In many respects, he is right.

Inheriting an economic crisis in 2008 like nothing since the Great Depression, President-Elect Barack Obama and his incoming chief of staff, Rahm Emmanuel, saw an opportunity. They knew the challenges of introducing policy change in normal times. When enough people feel secure in their wallets, freedoms, and health, those who want to stop change—"conservatives"—usually win. Obama and Emmanuel embraced the opportunity in the financial crisis not just because crises demand better leadership, but because they also allow more space for ambitious politics. Obama saw a window of opportunity that would quickly shutter and set about kick-starting the economy and delivering health care reform.[2]

By all accounts, today's converging economic, health, racial and climate crises dwarf anything we faced in 2008. 2021 may be the best moment for deep reform since the end of World War II, when most rules of today's international order—the multilateral governance and financial institutions, and legal and rights frameworks—were born.

That fact has most "conservatives" (those who prefer

stability to change, traditional power hierarchies to disruption, and the reliability of the past over the risk of a transformed future) deeply anxious, on both the left and right. Left-leaning conservatives, who self-describe in the U.S. as "moderates," particularly the wealthy, talk about "restoring" the way things used to be. They yearn for a more civilized politics where leaders were respected, and institutions trusted enough for citizens to spend less time protesting. They trust the neoliberal economic model that seemed to work well for enough people, even as it created a billionaire class and destroyed the planet for all of us. They had hoped to return to an economy, society and culture that might gradually heal racial and gender wounds.

Obama was right that his moment of opportunity would be short. By 2010, it wasn't just the Republican takeover of Congress that limited his progressive agenda. His own wealthy democratic supporters started to use their money to shore up the policies that enriched them, which led to a great economic divide over the next decade. Wealthy democrats supported cuts in food stamps, social security, and economic aid to other nations,[3] even though rank and file progressives and the general public wanted more of all these things.

In a July 2020 piece entitled "Why Do the Rich Have So Much Power?"[4] Paul Krugman shows how economic inequality expanded over the decade in part because of the obsessive attention that the super wealthy paid to cutting taxes and spending. It really wasn't until the post-mortems were done after the 2016 elections, followed by a raft of progressive wins in the 2018 mid-terms, that it became clear that Democrats had to harness both moderate and progressive energy to get back into power. Which is why, when it comes to economic policy, Democrats talk less about restoring the past economic order and more about transforming the policy agenda. With rising public anger about domestic economic, health and social injustice, and a failing global response to this economic crisis, climate change, and this pandemic, the range of policies acceptable to mainstream voters is moving to the left. And Moderates are worried.

Conservatives on the right are even more anxious. Not only are they witnessing the growing power of a redistributive political agenda that is targeting their pocketbooks, their political hold over institutions and their social norms, but Trump and political leaders on the right around the world—think Bolsonaro, Putin, Modi, and Johnston—are anything but conservative. Those leaders thrive off chaos and volatility, the kryptonite of conservatives. Look at nations with the most COVID-19 cases: by mid-September they were the U.S., Brazil, India, Russia, and Peru,[5] with India facing an economy that has shrunk more than any other during the pandemic, and the fastest rise in cases.[6] All governed by right-wing autocrats with a declared hostility both to conserving the status quo and to checks and balances.

The Power Switch Is Coming, for Worse or Better

Change is coming and so those who resist it—conservatives—are right to be anxious.

Economic and power inequalities have only become greater since the pandemic started. There is no reason to assume that those who have now accumulated power and wealth will not use this moment to seek to expand their power further.

That is what has progressive activist Naomi Klein so concerned. In *The Shock Doctrine*, she describes "disaster capitalism" as the economic liberalization and political capture that has driven the growth of extreme economic inequality. She argues that these forces use moments of crises to redistribute even more power to those who have too much. At this pandemic's outset, Klein warned activists that the virus was precisely the kind of "shock" to distract the public and allow the Trump Administration to bail out industries, exacerbate the economic inequality and climate crisis, and subsidize powerful groups like the airline, gas and oil industries.[7]

Now is the time, Klein argues, for American activists to fight for universal health care, child care, paid sick leave, higher taxes on corporations and on wealth. A more fair and just economy for all Americans. The conditions in the U.S. are ripe for a positive power switch. The pandemic is giving us a crash course on how connected these issues are and how enmeshed we are as a society. Even those with the privilege of being able to work at home and stay socially distant recognize that if health workers, package deliverers, the people in the food industry aren't safe, they won't be safe either.

We can imagine a progressive power switch in the U.S. after the 2020 elections, but what about in the wider world? Thirty years ago, an American shift to a more equal society and economy would have augured well for our planet. Today, with the rise of China and other nations, President Trump diminishing America's standing and credibility, the influence of multinational corporations on the global stage and multilateral cooperation in crisis, there is no inevitability that what happens in the U.S. will help to transform the global economy.

Some progressives dismiss the possibility of tackling reducing extreme inequalities of power and money. They are not resistant to change, only doubtful about the likelihood that we can shift well-established market patterns underlying much of these inequalities, or that the current crop of leaders is capable of driving this agenda. Their skepticism is easy to understand. Moreover, if massive wealth redistribution is hard while the pie is growing, surely it is even harder when the pie is shrinking at a record-breaking rate.[8]

The Stakes Are High

Three nightmares keep international activists awake:

Anti-democratic authoritarians from powers like Brazil, China,

India, Russia, and Turkey may gain more post-pandemic confidence to grab the moment of global uncertainty and rewrite rules in their favor. People from weaker democracies are already more likely to want army rule or autocrats today than they were a decade ago.[9] China is well positioned to use its economic muscle as creditor to the developing world to reshape financing, trade and economic relationships. Supplicant governments, devastated by the global economic shutdown, are likely to silence activism in exchange for economic forgiveness, partnership and the hope of recovery.

A second nightmare: private power fills the power void. Multinational corporations, seeing wounded politicians who proved themselves either disinterested or incapable of cooperating across borders, will recognize that the space and energy to lead the global economy now belongs to them. In service of an extractive shareholder model, and with ailing economies desperate to grow again, corporations will be well positioned to demand lower taxes, less regulation, and more corporate subsidies. As western corporations increasingly compete in an unregulated marketplace with Chinese, Russian, Indian and Brazilian corporations, they will squeeze workers and supply chains to extract more shareholder value, and extractive corporations will rush to plunder our remaining carbon and mineral resources to get economies moving again.

A third nightmare: Rules-based multilateral institutions lose their grounding altogether. The United Nations has never been more hamstrung and clearly in need of new ideas and different power dynamics. Crippled by a Security Council at war with itself, a decade of failed efforts to protect communities and bring peace to Syria, Libya, and other conflicts, it cannot muster the collective energy to lead us out of this crisis, despite having a well-respected Secretary General. Many will concur that Russia and the U.S. are no better guardians of permanent peace.

The International Monetary Fund, even with its new leadership, only managed incremental inroads to relieve the debts of developing countries hit by the crisis. Rather than canceling debt payments for all developing countries, they suspended them for a few, pushing off accumulating payments until 2022 when most countries, certainly in Africa, will face a wall of bond repayments and have far fewer tax revenues because of economic slowdown. The IMF's ability to draw on its global reserve of Special Drawing Rights was crippled by hostility from the U.S. to any economic multilateralism that might yield China more power in the IMF or oblige the U.S. to support any mechanism that might also benefit Iran, Venezuela and other adversaries that would have drawing rights.

The crisis in these multilateral institutions is apparent not just to the specialists, advocates and economic elites that engage in global economic transactions. The voting public is seeing the collective failure of joint leadership firsthand. They saw a U.S. President hold the UN Security Council hostage in his effort to disempower the World Health Organization, when his own agency, U.S.ID, argued the WHO was critical to fighting COVID-19.

Doomsday power switches are not hard to envision. Part Two of this book argues for activists grabbing the opportunity of this moment. Though the perils of inaction are great, so are the rewards for collective action.

Part Two

Inequality Crisis and Opportunity

Chapter 4

From an Inequality Virus to Coronavirus

Extreme economic inequality was tearing societies apart even before the pandemic. Just consider how unprepared most public health and human welfare systems around the world were to care for their populations. The pandemic did not just prey on extreme inequalities of power, it enhanced them, putting billions of people in every country in greater peril.

The Seeds of Today's Inequality

Time to get into some data. Many American progressives trace the birth of modern extreme economic and social inequality trends to the 1980s: when government "became the problem,"[1] neoliberal economics took undisputed primacy over U.S. and global economic policy, and the modern racist system of mass incarceration took off.[2]

From the fall of the Soviet Union until this pandemic, one set of economic assumptions has dominated multilateralism and public policy-making in most countries: economic growth is the rising tide that will lift countries and communities into prosperity. "Redistributing" what we already have, at least for American-trained economists, was morally questionable and intellectually vapid. Why focus on sharing the pie differently when by growing it, there would be more for everyone? With emerging economies like China, India and Ethiopia growing more than 5% a year, in recent decades, and official poverty numbers falling, the case for growth was strong.

Neoliberals touted deregulation, privatization, and lower taxes for the wealthy and corporations.

Average corporate tax rates globally fell from nearly 50% in the early '80s to 26% by 2015; the global average for top personal income tax rates fell from more than 60% to less than 40%.[3]

When the financial crisis hit in 2008, the redistribution of wealth, income, and power to the wealthy got even greater. In 2009, there were less than 800 billionaires in the world. By 2018, there were more than 2200, whose total wealth exceeded nine trillion dollars.[4]

At the same time, global corporate wealth rose by similarly astronomical figures. The Global Fortune 500 increased their profits by 156% from $820 billion in 2009 to $2.1 trillion in 2019,[5] far outstripping GDP global growth in the same period.

Where did corporate profits go? Oxfam's *Power, Profits and the Pandemic* report (September, 2020) found that between 2009 and 2019, S&P 500 companies spent $9.1 trillion on payouts to their shareholders—equaling over 90% of their profits.[6] In 2019, just before the pandemic struck, the 25 most profitable companies spent more than 120% of their earnings on shareholder dividends or stock buybacks.[7] In other words, they were taking on debt in order to pay out investors. Where did all this investor wealth go? Before the pandemic struck, close to 10% of all global wealth (more than $8 trillion) was sitting in tax havens doing nothing for anyone.[8] This was not just a waste.

This is a story about power. That tax havens exist and wealth taxes are low (less than 4% globally) is less about popular support for trickle-down economics than the fact that extreme wealth captures politics and makes it harder to redistribute the resources we already have.[9] As U.S. Supreme Court Justice Louis Brandeis famously said "We may have democracy, or we may have wealth concentrated in the hands of the few, but we cannot have both." Brandeis's zero-sum view of the world had been out of fashion during the "growth is all you need" years.

Some economic elites, as Anand Giridharadas recounts in *Winners Take All*, argue that their wealth and its power to do good did not come at the cost of others. It simply gave them more scope than the average Joe to make our world better. To be fair, some billionaires—think Bill Gates and George Soros—invest a huge chunk of their vast fortunes in trying to do just that. In 1994, Bill Gates became America's richest man with $9.4 billion.[10] Since then, he has given away more than $45 billion,[11] and still had $111 billion in July 2020.[12] Investment and tax rules being what they are, he literally can't give his money away fast enough.

Corporations are not so generous. While most engage in philanthropy or have corporate social responsibility funds that invest both in the communities impacted by their investments and in social programs that demonstrate a moral purpose for their staff, shareholders and the increasingly discerning public, the scale of those investments is pitiable. In 2017, while the U.S. lost $135 billion in revenue due to corporate tax dodging, corporate philanthropy was less than $20 billion.[13]

What might have happened before the pandemic? A decade of immense gains in wealth and corporate profitability might not have left us so unprepared for the pandemic. With only 4% of public revenues globally coming from wealth taxes, Oxfam estimated before the pandemic that a .5% increase in wealth tax for the richest 1% would have generated enough health care resources to save the lives of more than 3 million people and educate every child on the planet that was out of school—262 million children.[14]

Think about what those resources could have done to provide health and education resilience during the pandemic. If corporations had invested more profits in their workforces or made their supply chains more resilient and fairer, we might not have seen so many workers facing a crisis with no safety net. Instead, more than one in five of all workers worldwide were living in extreme or moderate poverty despite having employment before COVID-19. If corporations had paid more taxes on profits to governments where they worked, and governments had been committed to the welfare of their populations, there would have been more resources for front line health workers and humane levels of social protection for those shut into economic lockdown.

Why is extreme wealth such a bad thing? What's so bad about them having a few luxurious toys or different options for vacations? So, they get to watch sports from sky boxes while most folks are in the bleachers. As Michael Sandel reminds us in *What Money Can't Buy: The Moral Limits of Markets,* sky boxes hermetically seal the rich out from all the fun. What is wrong with corporations rewarding risks taken by shareholders and reinvesting in innovation? It is not just the wealthy who benefit from shareholder capitalism. The pension funds and 401(k)s of many workers hold savings in corporate shares. For many in white collar jobs, it's the only form of savings they have. Isn't it a good thing that shareholder value has increased? Isn't that why most Americans gave Trump more credit on managing the economy than just about any other issue.[15]

At the end of the day, in democracies, voters get to decide how much wealth and income disparity they are willing to accept. If inequalities grow too large, they can vote for redistributionist politicians. In the U.S., voters can choose Democrats over Republicans, Bernie Sanders over Biden, and Biden over Trump. And often many choose not to, either because they don't want more focus on redistribution and less on growth, don't trust that the politicians can deliver, or care more about other things. Many people look at extreme wealth and see possibility. "That could be me," they say, "and I would rather live in a world where that kind of wealth is possible than one where it isn't" and so they vote for systems that tolerate massive inequality, even if they are on the wrong end of the equation.

The maxim that the democratic compact between citizen and state is the best way to manage extreme inequality depends on two key assumptions: there are protections for vulnerable minorities who don't carry enough electoral heft, and there are protections against political capture by those with the money to make sure that all votes are not equal. Both of those assumptions have proven to be wrong.

Even before the pandemic spread around the world, it was becoming clear that electoral politics was failing for more and more people struggling to meet basic needs. Protesters no longer believed they could rely on the ballot box to fix these problems of economic inequality. They saw more and more political and economic power being held by fewer people. In country after country in 2019, economic "straws" broke the public's patience with the already vast economic gap between the richest and the rest. When the government tripled the price of bread in Sudan, it was overthrown after violent protests.[16] In Chile, where the 12 richest people have the same wealth as 25% of Chile's economy, a 4% rise in metro fares put activists on the streets and led to thousands of arrests and detentions.[17] In Lebanon, a tax on phone calls turned a quarter of the country's population into street activists.[18] In France,[19] Haiti,[20] Ecuador,[21] Iran,[22] and Guinea,[23] the catalyst for protests was fuel prices. In Iraq, it was the loss of basic services.[24] In India it was education fees.[25] In the world's most unequal region,[26] Latin America, "a rage brewed."[27]

The "development narrative" that economic growth would lift all boats felt increasingly hollow. Yes, we celebrated that extreme poverty had fallen from 1.9 billion in 1990, to 736 million by 2015, based on the World Bank $1.90 a day threshold. But $1.90 was a "scandalously unambitious benchmark,"[28] as the UN Special Rapporteur on extreme poverty found, and in any event, only possible because of rising incomes in China. Before the pandemic struck, three decades of growth had left more than 3.4 billion people living on less than $5.50 a day, only one crisis moment from destitution.

Americans had plenty of reasons to protest too. For thirty

years, they knew their economy was growing, but they weren't seeing the benefits at home. Average life span started to lag behind other developed countries.[29] The 2020 Social Progress Index found that of 163 countries it has been measuring since 2011, the United States saw the worst declines in that period,[30] and is now ranked 28, behind countries like Estonia and Greece.[31] Unlike Europe, the share of the economy going to workers dropped over the last 15 years. CEO-to-worker pay stretched to more than 40:1 — almost four times that of Japan and twice that of Canada. Federal minimum wage in 2018 was lower than Slovenia's and far below France, Britain, Canada, Germany and other developed countries.[32]

Then the Pandemic struck...

The pandemic may have landed first and worst on the general populations in China, Europe, and North America, but it inevitably concentrated on the people, communities and countries with the least capacity to fight it off. This created crises of health and hunger.

As a health pandemic, COVID-19 widened inequalities wherever it landed in 2020. Across urban slums in Asia, Africa, and Latin America where tens and often hundreds of thousands shelter on top of each other, social distancing, let alone a social safety net, were foreign concepts. When people did not get out to find work or food, the health crisis quickly became a hunger crisis. They had to risk infection and often police oppression to survive. With the combined public health budgets of the poorest eighty-five countries less than $160 billion — less than the combined wealth of the world's two richest men — health care workers had to take extraordinary risks, and hospitals and rural clinics were easily overwhelmed.

In Europe and North America, the disease also took its toll unequally. Health care workers, 76% of whom are women, were on the front lines;[33] as were those who care for the sick, children and the elderly. An Oxfam and Promundo poll found that in the U.S., daily house and care work increased drastically during the pandemic, especially for people of color. For Black, Latinx and Asian respondents, unpaid care work increased by more than 70%.[34] Cashiers (82% of whom are women), Uber and delivery drivers had no choice but to work. It hit the workers at meat processing plants in Brazil and the U.S., who were under-protected, though deemed essential, and who became vectors for the spread of disease. In England, despite having a National Health Service, mortality rates in the poorest areas were double those in rich areas.[35]

As a health pandemic in the summer of 2020, the virus claimed up to 10,000 lives a day globally.[36] Oxfam believes that even more people—12,000 a day—will die from hunger related to the unequal economic impacts of the pandemic.[37] The impacts will be especially deadly in "hunger hotspots" around the world, places like Yemen, Afghanistan and South Sudan. In Yemen, remittances dropped by 80% in the first four months of 2020 as workers lost jobs in the Gulf and borders and supply lines were closed in a country that imports 90% of its food. In the Sahel, herders have been unable to move livestock to greener pastures.

By October, the virus reached all 200 countries and put a quarter of a billion people at risk of acute hunger and risked putting twice that number back into poverty.[38]

And the Winners Are...

If we want to follow where money and power has gone during this crisis, and how both have been used to increase inequalities, we need look no further than the excess super-profits that corporations have made in 2020 and the shareholder windfalls that resulted for the extreme wealthy.

In a September 2020 report, *Power, Profits and the Pandemic,* Oxfam showed how the profits of large corporations have soared in 2020 despite the pandemic. It found that five tech companies, Microsoft, Google, Apple, Facebook and Amazon made $46 billion in "excess" profits in the first six months of 2020,—that's *more* profits than they made over the same period in previous years. Just six pharmaceutical companies expect to make about $12 billion in "excess" profits.[39] Who gains most from this windfall? The most prominent shareholders of these corporate giants are the world's billionaires, the 25 richest of which have increased their wealth by an average of more than $10 billion *each* since mid-March.[40] The shareholder-first paradigm has protected large corporations and their wealthy stock owners while the informal economy has been decimated, and workers have faced elevated health costs, cuts to pay, and job security risks.[41]

Latin America, already the world's most unequal region, minted a new billionaire every two weeks once the pandemic began, Oxfam found in *Who Pays the Bill* (July, 2020). The region's 73 billionaires made almost $10 billion a month through July of 2020, while more than 140 million people in the informal economy, nearly one in five in shanty towns, found themselves without social protection. Brazil's 42 billionaires increased their net worth by $35 billion between March and July. In the same period, Chile's seven richest increased their wealth by more than 25%.[42]

At the same time, the most vulnerable faced the brunt of the pandemic. In a region where one in three women are affected by gender-based violence, stay at home orders have led to an upsurge in violence. When Peru became a global hotspot of COVID-19 infection, and went into lockdown, 42% of Peruvians without bank accounts had to risk their lives to join crowded queues to get support. More than 5 million Venezuelans displaced in the region had neither a social safety net nor the ability to work. Tens of thousands risked their lives to go back to their homes across the Andes. Across Latin America and the Caribbean, 52 million people could be forced into poverty in

2020, setting back the fight against poverty there by 15 years.[43]

Thomas Friedman and Naomi Klein were right. Moments of massive disruption will create a power switch for better or worse. So far, that switch has hurt most people on the planet and benefited the super-elites of our broken economic system. Whether political leaders can now come together to agree on a broad economic reset that switches power back to where it belongs—with most of humanity—is the question with which I grapple in Chapter 5.

Chapter 5

Strategic Challenges for U.S. Activists

A host of challenges stand between activists and a progressive vision for our future: too many to cover in this short book. Many I don't touch on here—surveillance technology and the loss of privacy, how COVID-19 and artificial intelligence are changing the ways we work and live, the death of deference in politics. I draw the following seven challenges from my own experiences because each one presents a choice for American progressives. Consider where you agree and land on these choices:

1. Winning the Presidential election is only half the battle,
2. U.S. exceptionalism won't save us,
3. Americans knowing about global inequality does not mean they care,
4. Power games with China could destroy or repair America's global standing,
5. Vaccine inequality will be a real thing,
6. Surviving the collapse of old-school multilateralism, and
7. Youth activists aren't interested in old-school campaigning.

Challenge 1: The 2020 U.S. Presidential Election Was Only Half the Battle

With only 48 hours left in his Vice Presidency in January 2017, Joe Biden bared a torn heart at the World Economic Forum in Davos between his belief in a liberal international order that had yielded seven decades of American prosperity, and his concession that it had "deepened the rift between those racing ahead at the top and those struggling to hang on in the middle, or falling to the bottom."[1]

Four years later, President Biden faces a similar internal struggle, though in a different world. His moderate instincts will gravitate toward restoring the old order and its benefits, but he knows that going backwards is not a viable political strategy or leadership vision, nor can the U.S. assume the unipolar power it once had.[2] Which is one reason why he made so many commitments on the campaign trail to transform the American and global economy to deliver for more people. Will he come through on those campaign promises? Where will he spend his foreign policy capital?

A lot will depend on what American international activists do to put pressure on the Biden Administration and the U.S. Congress to prioritize those campaign promises. Before the pandemic hit the U.S. in March 2020, Elizabeth Warren and Bernie Sanders were leaning into frustrations about extreme inequality—corporate welfare, opulent wealth—and the power distortions that it brings. More moderate candidates, Harris and Biden among them, focused less on inequality and more on hope. Their "theory of change," like Obama's, was to unite progressives and moderates under a broad and positive tent. The politics of hope prevailed in the democratic primaries: With such a divisive narcissist in the White House, more Americans wanted an empath who understood their pain than a leader willing to wage the next fight against the superrich and powerful.

But this primary victory was not without a clear warning to Biden and Harris: to take the White House and deliver a Senate capable of passing a legislative platform, Biden could not simply show up as a sentient adult, offer hope and the promise that "I'm not him." While not being Trump may have been Biden's greatest asset, he soon saw he needed more than that to energize the kind of sweeping victory that will allow a deep reset of our national and global economy. Biden made clear in his Convention speech in August that he needed a transformative political and economic platform to get both moderates and progressives to the polls. He was tuned in to the world around him. Warren, Sanders, the rise of "the Squad,"[3] the growing power of Black Lives Matter, climate activism, and the Me Too movement embody the popular energy towards fighting inequality. Americans want more than just hope.

Having won, the task for international activists is to hold the new Administration to deliver on its promised power switch in 2021 and ensure that just as America aims to transform itself domestically, it transforms the role it plays in the world.

Challenge 2: Getting from Exceptionalism to Engagement

In "Missing America"[4] an excellent podcast broadcast just before the 2020 elections, Ben Rhodes, Obama's former speech writer, claims that the world had been missing America's leadership and wants it back. For him, American leadership is the special sauce between *The World as It Is* (2020) —his fascinating memoir of the Obama years—and how it ought to be. I am not so sure he is right, either about what the world wants or about how to generate activist energy in the U.S.

When I returned to Washington from my time in Afghanistan and Kenya just before the 2008 global financial crisis, internationalist activists, candidates and politicians often invoked the Marshall Plan and the defeat of the Soviet Union to inspire U.S. engagement overseas. American generosity and its commitment to a rules-based global economy and democratic international order had yielded a half-century of American power that had helped billions overseas and made the U.S. the shining city on a hill.

Even before Trump, the shift from a unipolar to multipolar world was in full swing. In 2008, when Obama went to the G20 for help in tackling the 2008 financial crisis (and got a commitment of $1 trillion from its members), he was asked whether he believed any more in American exceptionalism. He replied that American exceptionalism was probably no different than British or Greek exceptionalism and was pilloried back home for conceding America's primacy.[5]

Today, it has become clear to most, both at home and abroad, that the power of the U.S. is different. American power may never have been adequate to tackle global challenges unilaterally, but until recently, the indispensability of American engagement gave U.S. politicians an assurance: The world cannot move without us, so until our interests are met, we can wait, they thought. The comparative power of the American economy, media and military assured American politicians of relevance, if not prominence, in sorting out global challenges.

That equation no longer holds, and American politicians know it. If President Biden appeals to American exceptionalism, he knows he is on very different ground than when he made that appeal in 2012.[6] In 2017, only 12% of youth between 18–29 believed that the U.S. stands above other countries, and they were four times more likely than Americans over 65 to concede that "there are other countries that are better than the U.S."[7] One doesn't need a 2020 poll to know that this pandemic has further diminished American exceptionalism.

Trump may have been partly tapping into public cynicism about the costs and benefits of America's international engagement, but there is little doubt that his presidency also damaged American power. Surrounded by anti-institutionalists and isolationists like Stephen Miller, Peter Thiel, and Steve Bannon, the dealmaker in Trump was easily convinced that America should not be duped into costly foreign adventures or subsidizing public international goods with amorphous benefits back home. The Trump years decimated the rules and institutions on which the U.S. has relied for its global influence. Trump never saw a cooperative multilateral body or treaty that he didn't want to pillory. He treated the world as a zero-sum playing field for transactional deals from which he must extract short-term wins for the U.S. and credit for himself. As a result, other countries have less trust in U.S. multilateral leadership. Trump's America First turned into America Alone. And his domestic response to the pandemic is, for the first time in America's 200-year history, evoking "pity" around the world.[8]

This power reset is not lost on younger activists, and they don't want a return to American exceptionalism. But they do want engagement. Today's American activists start from a much deeper intuition about the relationship between power and social identity. They want more authentic and balanced relationships with citizens in other countries on which to rebuild human, fair, sustainable, and just economies and societies that work for everyone. In that direction, they envision the U.S. exercising its power more by example than by coercion, more through partnerships than the assertion of primacy and isolated self-righteousness. They want U.S. engagement in the world, not exceptionalism from it.

Challenge 3. Americans Knowing about Global Inequality Is Not the Same as Caring

Fighting inequality overseas at the cost of a healthier and fairer America is a campaign that progressive internationalists will never win. American voters may agree that economic unfairness overseas is a bad thing, but most care far more about their own immediate needs and domestic concerns. To the extent that Americans endorse financial reforms, they want that money and power to help them navigate their own financial crises. When the House passed a $3 trillion stimulus package in May 2020, to counter the economic downturn provoked by the pandemic, it allocated not one penny for the fight against poverty overseas. American politicians know those investments must be justified to voters at home. So how to convince U.S. policy-makers and corporate leaders that it is in the U.S.'s self-interest to invest deeply in reducing inequality overseas during and after this pandemic?

International activists need to build common cause with domestic activists around a shared agenda to redistribute global economic power. The activist movements in the U.S. today that are sweeping progressive politicians into office are about inequalities of race, gender, sexual identity and class. They are struggles to protect American workers and those 30 million claiming jobless benefits in the pandemic.[9] They are fights to protect homes from the ravages of fires and hurricanes intensified by climate change.

Progressive internationalists must demonstrate that the society and economy we want for Americans *depends* on reversing extreme inequality in other countries. We need to convince U.S. focused activists that by engaging on America's role in the world, they can advance their domestic struggles for justice. We should do that first by making the case for American soft power and reduced militarism, and second, by demonstrating that everyone wins from a healthier and fairer world.

First, progressive internationalists should challenge the kind of power we *don't* want the U.S. to exercise. Today, the U.S. military, still present in 149 countries around the world and deployed for combat in 14 countries,[10] reminds people everywhere that the U.S. is "the most warlike nation in the history of the world," as Jimmy Carter put it.[11] America's wars since September 11, 2001, have displaced 37 million people, refugees to whom we shut our doors.[12] Anti-war movements of the last 60 years, from Vietnam through Afghanistan and Iraq to today's Saudi-led war in Yemen have fought for less hard power. By putting more muscle into American soft power — more diplomacy and investments in crisis prevention, social protection and peaceful democratization around the world — the U.S. can lower burdens on our military and our national budget.

Relatedly, a failure to tackle extreme inequality overseas

will create even more pressure to use American hard power overseas. Because the pandemic divided countries even more, it is likely that the protests and instability of 2019 and 2020 may be a harbinger for what is to come in 2021 and beyond.

Second, we need to make a strong case that extreme inequality anywhere is a threat to us all. There has never been a better moment to make the case for interconnectivity, because there has never been a crisis like this—world wars included—that has interconnected our world so quickly. Within three months, a virus originating in Wuhan threatened indigenous communities in the Amazon. The virus pounded hubs of global connectivity: Rome, Madrid, London, New York. Voters know viscerally that a virus anywhere threatens people everywhere. I write this while on fourteen-day quarantine in Connemara. It was strange for our family to arrive in rural Ireland and find ourselves feared for having come from the capital city of the U.S., currently a global pandemic hotspot. While the economic pain from the crisis may ultimately be felt more in the south, it matters that the health crisis landed first and worst in the North. As activists we are engaging with a public that is feeling the pain of this crisis in deep ways, and they are looking for solutions.

Many Americans now believe that another pandemic will come after COVID-19 and understand that if national health systems lack the capacity, international support or mature political leadership, then a regional epidemic like Ebola in 2014 will become a global pandemic like COVID-19 and it will land unequally everywhere. (For more on this topic, see the companion book in the *Resetting Our Future Series: A Global Playbook for the Next Pandemic* by Anne Kabagambe.) We must use this window of interconnected consciousness to explain the need for a reset of our economies everywhere: better regulation of international corporations and their global supply chains, better international tax laws and debt cancelation programs will help develop healthier markets for American products and jobs for American workers, and at the same time, recover America's standing.

Challenge 4. Power Games with China Could Destroy or Repair America's Standing

For decades, China's rise has been reaching every corner of the globe. It now has more embassies than the U.S., doubling their diplomatic investments from 2011 to 2018, while Trump has tried to cut U.S. diplomatic investments by more than a third.[13] China heads up four UN agencies, while the U.S. leads one and rejects others (such as the World Health Organization) or fails to show leadership. At the outset of the pandemic, China held $1 trillion in U.S. treasuries and claims against debtor countries worth more than 5% of global GDP. Twelve countries rich in natural resources like Kyrgyzstan, Niger, and Zambia, or strategically positioned like Djibouti and Cambodia, owe more than 20% of their nominal economy in debt to China.[14]

In 2018, the U.S. Agency for International Development (USAID) created a "Clear Choice Framework"[15] that offered partner countries "the Path to Self-Reliance" as an alternative to deeper ties with China. It failed to stem Chinese influence. The Chinese Belt and Road Initiative, for all its lack of transparency,[16] dwarfs U.S. development expenditures and has grown China's influence with massive investments in Africa, South Asia, and Latin America at the expense of the U.S. influence in those regions.

In the early part of the pandemic, Trump sought to use the fact that the source of COVID-19 was in Wuhan to stir up anti-China sentiment, attacking the World Health Organization because of its engagement with China, and refusing to allow the IMF to issue new global reserves because China might benefit. His attacks only further diminished U.S. national standing.

Meanwhile, China launched an online messaging campaign

early in the pandemic to shape the narrative of its pandemic response and to offer an alternative for countries in their own response. While their lockdown was clearly effective, the means through which they achieved it and the offer they made to the world had sinister implications: a new contract between governments, business and the public that puts politics aside.[17] This offer, from an authoritarian regime that shut down activists in Hong Kong and detained more than a million Muslims in Uighur,[18] was chilling for global activists.

If activists agree that fighting global inequality requires a power switch from those who have too much, in authoritarian governments, corporations, and among wealthy elites, then the growth in China's power is a problem. Activists have already taken sides in the debate on whether healthy economies depend on political rights to remain economically inclusive—they do. As activists, we believe that the economic compact that reduces inequality depends on a political contract that democratizes power. Yet, as most China experts agree "The Chinese Communist Party sees no place for universal rights or global liberal norms."[19]

For Trump, and his Administration, the counter offer is zero-sum and backed by hard power. Since 2001 the U.S. has spent $6 trillion on warfare while China built its nation, pouring more cement in the three years from 2011–13 (6.4 gigatons) than America did in the entire twentieth century (4.4 gigatons).[20]

Progressive American internationalists want to offer the world a social contract fundamentally different from the Chinese model. One embedded in power distribution and making the playing field fair. Government "of the people, by the people, for the people" demands that societies are best driven, economically and politically, from the bottom up. Ironically, that soft power vision is partly what drove some support for Trump, and the ideas of Sanders and Warren: the promise to democratize information, money, and ultimately power and take back control from the establishment. Trump may have done more harm to American's equality than any president in history, but let's not fool ourselves—he convinced enough Americans that he was a champion who would redistribute power away from the wrong places to win the Presidency.

That frame—the democratization of power—offers a way forward for American activists to advance an alternative to China's political vision for the world. Despite the loss of America's global standing, its offer to the world matters, precisely because it is in a never-ending struggle against hegemonic control by establishment actors. The saving grace of the U.S. is that it doesn't just *concede* its own imperfection—it depends on it. America is built on the understanding that power corrupts, powerful institutions need constant correction and its power lies in government by the people, not by autocrats. If you want to understand how China thinks about that kind of power distribution, look at Xinjiang, Tibet and Hong Kong.

That is the U.S.'s comparative advantage in redressing economic, racial and gender inequalities. Although the American social contract has been deeply damaged by those inequalities, hope for the U.S. rests not in its politicians, but on the ability of institutions to withstand politicians and protect the power of its people. On that front, despite the damage left behind by the Trump Administration, the U.S. still has a better offer for the world than China.

Making the case for American soft power after Trump will be no easy task. Trump's polarizing leadership around the COVID-19 pandemic meant he was not just disinterested but incapable of unifying the international forces required to address the problem, and that fact alone, for some like the Berlin Office Director of the German Marshall Fund led to a "collapse of soft power of America."[21]

We may now need more humility, but that does not mean we cannot offer a vision for our world with profoundly American roots. We want the U.S. to compete on a different playing field: who is the better partner to developing nations? Who is the more constant and principled friend? Who identifies better the intersectional identities in societies and seeks to reach the most vulnerable? Whose corporations and investments leave communities more knowledgeable and confident, their systems more transparent, accountable and robust? That is the playing field we want for American internationalism. And that is the legitimate competition with China that we can embrace. Instead of vilifying Chinese students for seeking to steal American ideas and bring them home, as Secretary Pompeo did,[22] we should embrace them and say "You're welcome!" because our ideas about soft power and how it is used will ultimately transform your world too.

Challenge 5. Confronting Vaccine Inequality

It is quite possible that China will lead the discovery and distribution of the vaccines that end the COVID-19 pandemic. By late September 2020, they were contributing to five of the nine efforts in late phase-three trials,[23] with tens of thousands of people being tested in Brazil, Indonesia, Saudi Arabia, and Pakistan with these candidate vaccines. What happens if a Chinese vaccine is proven to be effective first? As one commentator fretted, the vaccine may be "the most important human resource in modern history," and China "will try to press their advantage in whatever ways they can,"[24] seeking to turn that advantage into power in current trade, economic, territorial, technology and military conflicts.

The Trump Administration is betting that it can guarantee a place at the front of the queue, either because Moderna, a U.S. company working with the U.S. Government and National Institutes for Health gets there first, or because it has provided funds to efforts like those being led by BionTech/Pfizer and AstraZeneca/University of Oxford, to guarantee vaccines get to the U.S. The dangers of vaccine nationalism tearing our world further apart is great.

The quandary and the opportunity are in the principles that drive vaccine rationing. The WHO first suggested countries should get vaccines based on the population size (which has the blessing and curse of being largely apolitical) and then argued that health workers should get it first, because they are on the front lines of the crisis. This does not make sense from an economic inequality perspective—such a principle would privilege rich nations who have much larger health systems and whose workers already get the protection of better personal protective equipment (PPE).

What principle should drive inequality activism? First, within countries, prioritizing low income communities with lower savings, higher dependency on wages, far less ability to "work from home," and greater likelihood to require public transportation to work will both achieve the greatest impact for them, and reduce the spread of the pandemic.[25] Second, because the health and economic consequences interact in a toxic cycle, the vaccine should go to the countries where poverty is greatest and health systems are weakest. That will not only save the most lives, but will in one simple decision, redistribute more power across humanity than has been done in our lifetimes. That is essentially the proposal of the Fair Priority Model proposed in September 2020, and for which inequality activists should fight before a vaccine is produced.[26]

Challenge 6. Surviving the Collapse of Old-School Multilateralism

Over the next four years, a global power switch will be impossible without robust multilateral institutions to govern corporate power, redistribute extreme wealth, eliminate tax havens, slow down climate change, manage escalating debt, and keep conflicts in check, but the institutions we currently have may be too sick to revive or rely upon.

The United Nations is creaking along in its seventy-five-year-old body, wishing its Sustainable Development Goals had more teeth, that nationalist factionalism had not paralyzed the Security Council, and donor governments would pay their dues and respond with funding so the UN could act. The World Health Organization became a lightning rod for tensions between the Trump Administration and everyone else. The International Monetary Fund, although it delivered some funds for debt relief,[27] has been unable to forge an agreement on Special Drawing Rights which could have released trillions of dollars into the global economy. The World Trade Organization, whose rules desperately need updating, canceled its June 2020 meetings in Kazakhstan, while countries around the world closed off supply chains or hoarded supplies to survive the pandemic. The High Commission for Refugees is coping with more displaced people than at any time in history, about 80 million,[28] and the Paris Agreement on Climate Change remained moribund without the U.S. and will be too little too late if the U.S. merely reinstates its pre-Trump commitments. Even the newer multilateral institutions may be terminally ill—the G7 didn't even meet at the head of state level in this crisis year, and the G20, created precisely to deal with global economic crises, barely agreed joint statements by the fall of 2020[29] and largely failed to deliver new funding in to the global system.

Trump's false choice that "the future does not belong to globalists" but to "sovereign and independent nations"[30] has deeply wounded every multilateral institution with which he has engaged. He fed American doubts about multilateral engagement. His allergy to solving global public challenges resonated with enough Americans in 2020, just before the pandemic, that most were satisfied with the U.S. position in the world (and 85% of Republicans were satisfied).[31]

How to recover American confidence in multilateral

cooperation? William Burns, President of the Carnegie Endowment for Peace believes that the U.S. should "reinvent" itself with some humility—build a "patchwork of arrangements, with coalitions of like-minded states at its core, which the U.S. is still better placed than any other country to assemble."[32] That may be a realistic first step. Even a forward-leaning Biden Administration cannot revitalize existing multilateral institutions without first building momentum and credibility. As I propose in Chapter Six, it would be a lot wiser to focus on putting in place new funding mechanisms and new agreements with like-minded partners that deliver real change for the most vulnerable and reestablish America's moral standing through selecting the right early wins.

Challenge 7: Youth Leaders Aren't Interested in Old-School Campaigning

Early in 2019, a group of Oxfam campaigners from around the world gathered in Mexico City to reflect on emerging trends in international activism. The energy we saw was in climate campaigning: Greta Thunberg, a Swedish teenager, had helped to inspire school walkouts and marches all over the world. Young people were organizing to denounce the false promises of governments to "grow" communities out of crises. They were outraged at the unfairness of climate impacts as they witnessed surging migration flows and escalating water and land conflicts. Many saw themselves taking up an existential fight for their own lives. In affluent countries more to blame for the climate crisis, Extinction Rebellion was capturing young imaginations by committing to civil disobedience in Britain, Australia, Ireland, Germany, the Czech Republic and elsewhere.[33]

Oxfam invited some young climate campaigners to join us by video to talk about how they were organizing. I asked a young Belgian how they had found a way to join a global effort, create a basic organizing structure, reach out to students all over their country and then shut down many of his countries' schools in a climate protest, raising the hackles and fears of their government. "Oh," he replied, "you don't understand, we started more than six weeks ago!" I remember the looks of my Oxfam colleagues as we raised our eyebrows at each other. Someone laughed nervously. Organizing the Belgian chapter of a global effort kickstarted by a teenage Swede with no infrastructure, no resources, no declared base of supporters, was phenomenal—it can take Oxfam months and sometimes longer to lay the foundation for a global campaign.

Black Lives Matter and Me Too are American inequality campaigns that became global because young people all over the world connected instantly with American struggles against police brutality and sexual assault and harassment. America is still the first reference point for many activists who "want to make some noise and get in good trouble, necessary trouble" as John Lewis said before he died.[34]

Today's young global activists are not waiting for broadcasts or marching orders from the traditional northern centers of civic activism—Europe and the U.S. UN Secretary General Antonio Guterres believes that "young people are leading the fight against inequality, discrimination and division..."[35] In his new book *How to Fight Inequality and Why that Fight Needs You* (September, 2020), Ben Phillips shows how young activists all around the world are picking up the baton from the great organizers against inequality and injustice of the past in the U.S. and around the world and redistributing power even as you read this. But it was also a sign of what's possible now. Young people move faster, make connections easier and are willing to demand big change. They are not stuck in the "politics of the possible"; they are not pleased to see the world "as it is." As Greta Thunberg warned "the world is waking up. And change is coming, whether you like it or not."

Chapter 6

To Switch Power, Follow the Money

If international activists want 2021 to contribute to a socially just power switch that really matters to the poorest half of humanity, we need to follow the money. Why? First, look at what is driving most inequality protests globally (see Chapter 4) and in the U.S. (see Chapter 5). That's where public energy is. People want concrete economic help with health, education, and unemployment protection. Second, redistributing money *is* a power switch: Today's extreme wealth and the political power it brings stops democratic and economic systems working effectively. That was a core finding from Oxfam's foundational research in *Working for the Few: Political Capture and Economic Inequality* (2014).[1] Third, if our deeper goal is to redistribute power, it is a clear and measurable way to make a difference on *both* ends of the spectrum: taking money from the extreme wealthy reduces their power over others; spending that money on social protection puts power into the hands of those who need it—a double win in terms of power redistribution. Finally, when trying to build political momentum, there is greater potential for early policy wins, because public funds always *have* to flow. For this reason, international activism in the U.S. often focuses on the federal budget. It is not just that money matters to fight inequality and poverty. Even when political gridlock is at its worst, governments must agree on budgets, and in deciding how that money is spent, they often make decisions about other things—a threat and opportunity in real time.

In this chapter, I look at the opportunities to reshape the flows of money as the pandemic subsides: where public money should come from and how it should be spent to tackle global extreme inequality.

Where will the resources come from?

The pandemic is going to increase inequality between wealthy nations that can raise taxes, print money, afford more debt and stimulate their own economies, and those with weak tax bases, high debt payments and few social services to start with.[2] Activists who want to reduce global inequalities in countries around the world should focus on three things: stop money leaking from the communities and countries where it is most needed; second, create new money while adhering to global monetary norms; and third, shift more money from wealthy countries to those in greater need. Each of these can redistribute both money and power, at different scales, timelines and impact.

Begin here: Stop Money and Power Leaking from Developing Countries:

Global economic leaders—think G20 countries and the IMF—could agree to radically shift power and resources to the right places by leaving wealth where it is being created in poorer countries. They can do this through debt cancelation and by changing global tax rules.

Debt Cancelation: Debt cancelations are an immediate transfer of wealth and power when done in the right way, with creditors absorbing costs. Instead of interest payments going from cash starved governments to bilateral creditor governments (like China and the U.S.), to the IMF or World Bank, or to private creditors and investors, debt cancelation releases funds for cash strapped governments that can be spent immediately on health and hunger.

At the outset of the pandemic in March 2020, Oxfam estimated that 45 countries were spending more than 400% of their health care spending in debt repayments, robbing them of the funds they needed to prepare for what was to come and began to work with other organizations to build support for debt relief.[3] The IMF and some donors recognized that debt relief was perhaps the best way to redistribute wealth, but could not find the political muscle or courage to cancel debts outright. Instead, debt payments were suspended for some countries until 2022, a year when many African countries will face a wall of bond repayments.[4] Some governments who were offered debt suspension, like Kenya, refused to take it, fearing a loss of future credit if powerful private ratings agencies downgraded them. How can any government responsibly increase expenditures in social protection, food security, education or health today if it is going to face huge repayments tomorrow?

A 2021 power switch should focus on getting the G20 and the IMF to cancel debts of all developing countries, including bilateral, multilateral and private debt. The costs of cancelation should be absorbed by creditors and aid, not by new forms of debt. There should be a moratorium on credit agencies lowering their ratings for any government taking debt relief; and a global agreement to regulate how private creditors step into the debt market place to profit from relief of public debts. Western countries should push for an agreement with China around the terms and transparency of debt repayments so that developing country governments are not playing creditors off each other in a race to the bottom.

The key targets for this case are the IMF and the G20 governments. The official action forcing moments will occur when the Saudi Arabian government hosts the G20 heads of state (in person or virtually) in late November 2020, with Italy hosting in 2021 and India in 2022. The other significant action forcing moment is when the Ministers of Finance gather for the spring and fall meetings of the IMF and the Fund each year.

The Biden Administration should not wait for these moments but use them to garner more support for an ad hoc debt cancelation initiative. This level of ambition will be necessary from the U.S. if it is to convince China—the world's largest creditor—to translate its current moratorium on debt repayments by the G77 low income countries[5] into something more ambitious and lasting. Without showing leadership on multilateral debt and its own bilateral debt, there is little hope that the U.S. will convince China to work together to stabilize the global economy. Both countries must use every instrument at their disposal to show how seriously our global economy needs a reset if it we are to avoid a decade of economic despair for billions.

Tax Reform: The other way to leave money in countries and economies is to ensure that taxes are paid where economic activity occurs and wealth is created. Before the pandemic, globally, tax avoidance was diverting 40% of foreign profits to tax havens.[6] According to the IMF, profit shifting by corporations was costing governments more than $500 billion a year—$200 billion of that leaving developing countries.[7] The wealth of the richest individuals was being taxed at less than 4%, often because wealth left poor and rich economies alike. More than $7.6 trillion ended up in tax havens.[8]

Once the pandemic hit, talk of growing the tax pie rather than slicing it differently in these moments was not going to cut it. Global tax revenues are likely to go down in this pandemic by even more than the 11.5% they experienced from 2007 to 2009.[9] Corporate tax revenues will dry up along with their supply chains, consumption taxes will drop, and personal income tax will tank as unemployment rises. And this will happen to a global tax system that was not operating well before the pandemic.

Going into this economic and health crisis, Oxfam was working with groups both in the global north (like the Patriotic Millionaires in the U.S. and the global Tax Justice Network based largely in the UK) and in many countries to mobilize public and policy-maker attention of the need for national and global tax reform.[10] At the national level, some of Oxfam's greatest successes has been highlighting the tax avoidance of oil, mining and gas companies and getting governments to pass or strengthen their financial oversight, transparency and tax laws by working with local partners to build national movements.[11] During the pandemic, Oxfam has been working with leading academics like Jayati Ghosh, Jose Ocampo, Thomas Picketty, Gabriel Zucman, and Joe Stiglitz, and activists in both the north and south supporting the Independent Commission for the Reform of International Corporate Taxation (ICRICT) to push for broad based tax reform.[12]

A 2021 Power Switch on Global Taxes should include a new effort through the United Nations to create a global tax authority that can regulate global corporate tax and the use of international tax havens by wealthy individuals. This should be a centerpiece for the 2021 UNGA; an OECD led agreement to oppose a 25% minimum effective corporate tax rate to stop base corporations shifting their profits and countries engaging in a never ending tax competition that races to rob the national treasuries of other countries of precious resources and publication of country by country reports of taxes paid for all corporations that get state support; national efforts, particularly in the U.S., to impose higher taxes for large firms with excessive rates of return during this pandemic; fresh commitments regarding taxes on international carbon use, arms trades, and financial transactions to generate public funding; and the publication of all offshore wealth so that nations can adopt more progressive wealth taxes.[13]

Direct New Money towards Countries Fighting Inequality

When a domestic economy runs into a financial crisis, leaders have other options besides taking on debt from others—they can print money—which may cause inflation or lower the value of their currency—or release funds from their own national reserves (if they have them).

Something similar can be done on a global scale. The IMF coordinates a global reserve which it calls "Special Drawing Rights" (SDRs). Members of the IMF agree to issue SDRs which can be drawn down by governments in allocations tied to the size of their economies. The currency allows the IMF to total the national reserves of member countries and allocate funding accordingly. It is a fast and powerful way to inject new funding scale to where it is most needed.

Once the economic consequences of the pandemic became clear, IMF members quickly began to consider issuing SDRs to allow governments to access global reserves to meet urgent needs. They looked at two ways to do this. The less ambitious approach is to reallocate existing SDRs from economies that are not using their allocations to countries most in need.[14] This can provide temporary relief, particularly if it comes in the form of grants not loans and is offered not just to low-income countries but those middle-income countries where the pandemic has massive potential to widen inequalities. The more ambitious approach is to issue new SDRs that will allow all countries to access more funding. One U.S. legislator, supported by Oxfam and other organizations, has proposed a $3 trillion issuance of new SDRs—about the level the global economy will contract in 2020.

The Trump Administration moved to block these efforts for several reasons: first it would have opened up a financial lifeline to IMF members that are U.S. adversaries like Iran and Venezuela; second, an increase in global reserves through SDRs, based on the current size of national economies would have changed the voting power of IMF members, redistributing power from the U.S. to China; and finally it would have demonstrated the value of multilateral cooperation for a Trump administration that has declared its hostility to anything other than zero-sum "deals" for the U.S.

A Biden-Harris Administration reversal of this policy would

be a powerful statement of revitalized multilateralism. A 2021 power switch on global reserves would allow countries to reallocate their reserves to those most in need including both low- and middle-income economies, in the form of grants not loans; and issue new SDRs at a scale that can offset the global economic contraction—at least $3 trillion.

Redistribute Power through Better Development Finance

Increasing Foreign Aid is probably the form of international money redistribution that has gotten most Northern activist energy in the past four decades and received the greatest backlash. Since the 1980s Band Aid campaign (which drew the world's attention to "a biblical famine" in Ethiopia) Northern founded humanitarian organizations like Oxfam, Save the Children and CARE and anti-poverty advocacy groups like ONE have known that by joining together with others, they could put real pressure on donor governments and publics to increase foreign assistance. Though public support for foreign assistance may thin out in tough budget eras and electoral campaigns, it has grown steadily over the decades off the back of campaigns like Make Poverty History.[15] At least until recent years, where it has remained flat at about $165 billion since 2014, it was one of the areas where activists could claim real success in redistributing money from rich to developing countries.

As the pandemic crippled donor economies, commitments to international aid have floundered. Richer economies who delivered stimulus packages for their own economies have failed to increase their overseas investments, leaving developing country governments, the United Nations and many INGOs struggling for resources to meet basic needs. Even progressive democrats in the U.S. like Nancy Pelosi have steadfastly refused to include emergency funding for overseas aid, knowing that many Americans are skeptical about foreign aid at the best of times, and are particularly focused on their own needs now. Without a visionary internationalist leader in the White House, American contributions to the global economic crisis have been pitiful. Other traditional leaders have also pulled back: the UK government, (traditionally one of the strongest champions of aid) collapsed its prestigious Department for International Development into the Foreign Office in the middle of the pandemic. These recent failures of leadership have created the kind of aid crisis that may offer a new opportunity for a power switch in the quality and quantity of aid.

Activists who want to see public finances increased should focus on two ideas:

Shift the range on the level of aid funding required. In 2020, with northern economies contracting, it has been impossible to ramp up traditional forms of foreign assistance with old activist strategies and arguments. Although half a billion people are at risk of falling back into poverty, wiping out a decade or more of progress in some regions, donors have failed to respond. There will be a moment in 2021, however, when the pandemic is increasingly under control or a vaccine is found and distributed, when governments are going to want to reshape and reenergize their international relationships and the multilateral institutions on which they depend. The transformation towards a new kind of international rules-based order which distributes power fairly will require development financing at scale as a core element. In *Dignity Not Destitution* (March, 2020), Oxfam estimated that global foreign assistance would have to triple — to about $500 billion a year — to contribute meaningfully to the economic and health inequality costs of this pandemic. It is critical that activists don't settle for the politics of the possible in that moment. The goal should be to shift public debate and the range of what politicians are considering in terms of the scale.

Create and champion new purpose based global funds to support recoveries that reduce inequality in health and in education. One lesson of the past 15 years is that generic calls for more aid land less well with politicians and the general public than more purpose-built initiatives. In this century, relative success stories in aid have included PEPFAR to fight the HIV/AIDS pandemic, the Global Alliance for Vaccines and Immunization (GAVI), the Coalition for Epidemic Preparedness Innovation (CEPI), the Global Fund to Fight Aids, Malaria and Tuberculosis, and the Millennium Challenge Corporation. Purpose built initiatives dedicated to measurable results that can be defended by politicians and understood more easily by the voting public. Two new initiatives that could garner such support in the recovery from this pandemic are a Global Fund for Public Health,[16] and an idea being proposed by Oxfam—a Global Social Protection Fund.

Where should resources be spent?

Perhaps the most damaging victory of neoliberal economics was to starve public investment in areas proven to reduce inequality: Health, education, social protection and creating economic opportunity for vulnerable and traditionally marginalized groups. The unique character of this pandemic has brought home the importance of strong expenditures in these areas. With health systems overwhelmed, more than a billion children out of school, two billion informal workers now vulnerable and the burden falling disproportionately on women and people of color in country after country, the need for and political possibility of an expenditure reset in 2021 may never have been greater in the last seventy-five years.

If the goal is to redistribute as much power as quickly as possible to the largest number of people, then the focus for activism in 2021 should be on the two issues at the top of most people's minds in most countries: health and hunger.

Three commitments to health investment and reform rise above all others: the free distribution of a vaccine, a massive scale up of funding for public health in the developing world, and a recommitment to free public health care for all, in both the north and south.

International activists should focus on vaccines not just for health reasons, but because the discovery of an effective vaccine could disrupt power dynamics either in dangerous or healing ways. It may be "the most important human resource in modern history," and lead to a violent switch of power towards those who control it.[17]

It is critical that activists everywhere fight for the vaccine to be manufactured, distributed and made available free of charge to the most vulnerable all around the world. Pharmaceutical companies must not be allowed to hoard or stockpile vaccines or distribute them only to the highest paying countries and customers while the pandemic remains. We must confront and shame governments, including our own, who engage in vaccine nationalism or who want to use the power of controling the vaccine to strengthen their global power. Consider how China might act after being attacked by the Trump Administration if it discovers an effective vaccine first and uses it to rebalance global economic rules of trade, investment and finance.[18]

As soon as we have a vaccine that has been adequately tested, and proven effective, it should be made patent free so it can be produced at cost in as many countries as necessary to reach everyone. Donor funding should go towards ensuring distribution reaches the most vulnerable, who often cannot be socially distant, are facing economic crises from lockdowns or are on the front lines of risk of infection because of the nature of their work—in the health sector, the care economy or as front line "essential" factory or service workers.

Second, we need governments to commit to increase investments in public health to help countries be better prepared for the next health crisis. Oxfam argued early in the pandemic that at minimum, rich countries needed to find $160 billion— enough funding to double the health expenditures of the world's 85 poorest countries. Developing country governments themselves must prioritize health care. When a country like Ethiopia, which has seen double digit growth figures year on year, still spends less than $2 per person per year in its health budget, its little wonder they are underprepared for health crises.

Finally, in wealthy countries, we must achieve adequate public health care for everyone. Perhaps no issue has divided Americans more in the past twenty years. As the Canadian anthropologist Wade Davis noted in *COVID-19 and the End of an American Era*[19] when a wealthy Canadian goes to a supermarket, she knows that her health care is the same as the cashiers' and the prime minister's. That fact strengthens the social fabric of their democracy in ways that Americans have not been able to call upon in this crisis. This pandemic has woken Americans up to the reality of a deeply unequal health care system which is why this issue is a core element of the progressive platform for reform. In the wake of this pandemic, activists must not let go of the right to quality public health care for all.

Social protection against hunger: More people will die from hunger in this pandemic than from the health crisis, Oxfam reported in July 2020.[20] The problem is not a lack of food. It's the fact that families in extreme poverty have to cut back on spending. As the New York Times Reported in September "the pandemic has reinforced basic economic inequalities, none more defining than access to food."[21]

What should activists do? Most urgently, we need to ensure that governments and humanitarian agencies get food and hard cash to those whose lives are at risk now. With donors pledging just a fraction of need—9% by July—the global food system deeply skewed towards powerful agriculture traders, food corporations and supermarkets, smallholder producers cannot meet need, particularly as a climate crisis is increasing food security in all the hunger hotspots and traditional food baskets.[22] Hundreds of millions face hunger particularly in the world's hunger hotspots from Afghanistan to Yemen.

The first responsibility for social protection lies with national governments who are accountable to protect the most vulnerable in their societies. As the pandemic has revealed the vulnerability of work, employment and current economic models, more and more leaders are going to turn towards universal social protection systems which guarantee that no one—citizens, residents or undocumented migrants—falls below a social floor in terms of health and hunger.

Relying on the national political will of every government won't be enough. Those facing severe hunger in 2021 are going to need cash to purchase the food they need. The United Nations, with its partners, wants to distribute $90 billion in emergency cash payments to 700 million of the most vulnerable in the form of social assistance programs or where they don't exist or don't have capacity, through humanitarian relief programs. Activists need to make sure these funds are prioritized.

But we need something more. Instead of waiting for future economic catastrophe to devastate more vulnerable communities and the UN to pass the begging bowl, donor governments need to agree on some form of global safety net that protects the most vulnerable when climate, pandemics, conflict and inequality conspire to leave vulnerable communities without basic social protection. If the Biden Administration were to work with others to create a new global fund for social protection to help the extreme poor survive shocks, it would be just the kind of jump-start that multilateralism needs.

Conclusion

Actions for International Activists to Consider

I hope we now agree on two things. First, our world needs a power switch if we are going to reverse extreme inequality, and second, international activism *might* be relevant to that power switch, but activists will need to be honest with themselves and strategic with others to make a difference.

What are the choices and practical actions to consider if you want to help shape that power switch in the coming months and years? Here are some reflections I've taken away from my own activism. Chew on them and let me know what you think at RedistributePower@gmail.com.

1. *Change the View from President Biden's Policy Window*

The "Overton Window" describes the range of policies politically acceptable to the mainstream population at a given time.[1] They are the policy options that a politician can recommend without appearing too radical. Reading about Joe Biden as Vice President in Ben Rhodes *The World as It Is: A Memoir of the Obama White House* and watching the Presidential campaign closely, one senses that Joe Biden always seeks the Overton Window for his solutions. His strengths and weaknesses are his fierce loyalty to what mainstream America wants from him. That's an important fact for activists because fighting against global inequality means you can't just try to win on policies that are already acceptable to the mainstream population today. We have to change the terms of debate—what the American public cares about—so that the Overton Window shifts towards fighting inequality overseas. We need to change President Biden's view.

The way to do that is to know when to be *manifestly unreasonable* in the proposals we use to organize public energy, not to achieve a specific outcome, but to change the Overton

Window. This is hard for professional and institutional activists: We gain precious credibility and access by being reasonable, and sometimes mildly difficult. When our proposals cause political eye rolling, they can be dismissed.

If we are to convince the Biden Administration to help reset global economic rules and institutions, proposing reasonable solutions won't be enough. As Ben Phillips tells it in his new book drawing lessons from the history of inequality activism, Martin Luther King knew that "Those fighting inequality had not only to overcome this pressure from others but also to overcome their own internalized 'fear of being nonconformists' and be willing to be not merely a thermometer that recorded the ideas and principles of popular opinion but a thermostat that transformed the mores of society.'"[2] If we want politicians to care more about inequality overseas, it is time to turn the heat up with the U.S. public.

When speaking to foreign aid levels, ending tax havens, setting up a global fund to protect the most vulnerable, don't always ask for what you think you can get, demand what's needed. Even if you don't get it, if you can build public support for your idea, you will change the window of what's possible.

2. Delivering Grassroots and Grass-tops Power

A new Administration and Congress facing multiple challenges in 2021 will invest in fighting global economic inequality only if it sees both grassroots and grass-tops energy behind that agenda. The power of grassroots activism comes from local level movements, collective action and voter muscle. Grass-tops activists cultivate influential individuals whose power comes from their positions, access, wealth, fame or following.

Building a grassroots campaign in the U.S. to fight economic inequality overseas is something no organization can do alone. Large international development and humanitarian organizations with campaigning capacity like CARE, World

Vision, Catholic Relief Services, Mercy Corps, International Rescue Committee, Save the Children, Oxfam and Plan have millions of grassroots supporters around the U.S. with whom they already run content rich advocacy agendas to advance their missions. Advocacy organizations like Move On, Amnesty International, ONE, Win Without War, Vote Vets and Results also have huge supporter bases in the U.S. These organizations share values and a common vision to protect and support the world's vulnerable people, and work together all the time on various issues, yet it is no simple task for them to agree on a common platform or shared campaign to deliver their grassroots power. During the primary season of the 2020 Presidential campaign, Oxfam America worked with more than two dozen groups whose combined social media platforms reached tens of millions of Americans to get candidates to commit to reengaging the "U.S. in the World" in more responsible ways to tackle income inequality, climate change, conflict, the refugee crisis, and gender inequality.[3] Building a big tent with grassroots power meant keeping the agenda broad. Even then we reached some, but not all the candidates.[4] As the next Administration and Congress shape their agenda, these groups will have to determine whether they can once again agree a broad goal that will allow them to demonstrate their grassroots power to the next Administration and Congress.

To build grass-tops power, groups like Patriotic Millionaires have found a way to bring progressive rich people together to demand more taxes on *themselves*. With their heft as political donors, the members of Patriotic Millionaires have given courage, support and funding to progressive U.S. politicians to prioritize tax reform and they use their unique convening power to great effect. The U.S. Global Leadership Coalition has made an artform out of bringing influential actors across the defense, diplomacy and development worlds to shore up Congressional support for overseas development funding. The Modernizing

Foreign Assistance Network brings together experts to whom Administrations (including the Trump Administration) often appeals to advance their agenda. Oxfam America's Sisters on the Planet Initiative gathers progressive women leaders with relationships to Members of Congress to advance our issues in targeted lobby days. Many of the development organizations above are also supported by celebrities, boards of directors and other influential supporters, and use that power to deliver grass-tops influence on their agendas.

With this wealth of grassroots and grass-tops strength and the multiple crises facing a new Administration and Congress, the challenge for international activists and convening bodies like Interaction will be to agree a broad agenda and then let each player speak to their issues so that collectively we take the opportunity in this global crisis for the U.S. to contribute to a power shift.

While these great groups are going to be necessary to make that power shift positive, I've met no one who believes that the groups we have today are enough for the coming moment. As an activist pushing for the right kind of power shift, you will have to choose how and where to spend your time: joining existing movements or building new initiatives and networks; in grassroots work building up the kind of local groundswell of support for U.S. re-engagement in the world, connecting to communities overseas, and seeking to build support for the specific policy wins that are laid out in Chapter 6, or as a grass-tops influential who can use your networks, access, fame, wealth, or social-media following to generate more political support for a progressive agenda.

3. Great Campaigns Translate Knowledge into Power Through Killer Facts

Effective activists are more like marital counselors than medical school professors. They focus less on what you know, and more on what you care about. They understand that real power comes when people choose change for themselves. Good facts—at Oxfam we call them "killer facts"—do both things. When you hear that a few of the world's wealthier countries with 13 percent of the world's population are buying up more than 50 percent of the vaccine doses,[5] it can change both what you know and feel about that injustice. When one hears that Jeff Bezos could pay each of his 875,000 employees a $105,000 bonus, and still have more money than he had when the pandemic began,[6] that makes us want to do something to regulate his wealth. Good research is essential for a persuasive progressive policy agenda but translating research into resonant killer facts may be even more important for converting knowledge into power. In many organizations, there are those with a knack for creating killer facts that explain injustice in powerful ways. Find those people, nurture their skills and unleash their potential.

4. When Dealing with Powerful Institutions and People, Be a Critical Friend

Half the battle in campaigning against target corporations or governments is to stir up internal debates within those institutions so that they also demand change from within. If our campaigning unites every employee, member or supporter of a target corporation or government against our cause, we will almost always fail. How do you foster or support internal debate? Irit Tamir, Oxfam America's Private Sector Director, believes the key is to be a "critical friend" of the corporations we seek to influence, and wrote a good article about it.[7] Essentially, it means this: When you criticize, do so with evidence and a fairness that doesn't allow those who disagree to dismiss you as ideological. When you form friendships or find common cause with an institution or actor you want to influence, never get so close as to compromise your legitimacy or ability to challenge that target on an issue of power distribution. It's a great approach for activists facing any public or private powerful target whose policies or practices you want to change.

5. Know When to Be an Orchestra and when to Jam

When I first started working as an activist, the early global campaigns against poverty were masterpieces of choreography and harmony. Activists synchronized actions across the world to deliver a power switch in a single moment. Perhaps the zenith of harmonic campaigning was when Phil Collins flew on Concorde from London to Philadelphia so we could all sing "We Are the World" to do something about Ethiopia's famine. Many big global campaigns since then have been about hitting targets at the same time with the same actions—the G7 or G20 heads of state, multiple corporations. When orchestra-like campaigning works, it is powerful. Each January, as fur-clad elites gather in Davos, Switzerland, Oxfam publishes a report about disparities of extreme wealth and poverty, and makes a united call to tackle inequality, which is covered by thousands of media outlets around the world. But that kind of moment has its challenges: great orchestras need a conductor. Someone in charge. Activists working across organizations and contexts are less and less interested in having one command center. Orchestra campaigning also assumes the same ask, delivered in the same way will deliver an outcome that everyone wants.

There are still important opportunities for orchestra campaigns, but increasingly, a different form of global activism is emerging. Campaigners working on issues may agree on a broad theme or target, but as they work with partners and across different contexts, they tailor their activism to take different positions and strategies—more like jamming than being in a controlled space.

Oxfam's efforts around the Commitment to Reducing Inequality (CRI) Index is an example of "this kind of looser" campaigning. The CRI Index which we launched at the Annual

Meetings of the World Bank and IMF in October 2020[8] compares government commitments to reducing economic inequality in 150 countries, but it's designed to be useful to campaigners who may have different targets and different campaigning approaches. In one context, activists may use the CRI in the fight to change taxes on corporations or individual wealth, while in another it will be used to fight for more health or education expenditures or to reduce gender pay gaps. The overall theme is the same—reduce economic inequality, but the contributions by campaigners are much more organic, less controlled and a different kind of harmony.

6. A Last Thought: Being the Change Is Hard but Worth It

International activism has changed in recent years in part because of how power works *within* activist movements. Campaigns that were once conceived and designed centrally, are now co-created with no clear leadership. Who told English Premier League footballers to kneel in solidarity with American Black Lives Matter activists? No one. As technology has evolved, so too has the power over content and tactics. Today's campaigners do less planning and more adaptation, less broadcasting of core brand messaging, and more dialogue; less waiting for a "conductor" to lead, and more time being leaderful together.

All of this is keeping activism fresh and engaging. And some of it has been driven by a transformation of power dynamics *within* institutional activist spaces. At Oxfam, we have been through our own journey. Having been publicly shamed for the worst form of power abuse—taking sexual advantage of earthquake survivors in Haiti who were ostensibly there to help[9]—we resolved to transform ourselves as a family. Since then, Oxfam has made huge strides in trying to "be the change" it wants in the world. It embraces feminist principles in everything it does, seeks to be more honest about its past, and thoughtful about its own power. It is on a journey to become deeply anti-racist and to grow beyond its roots as a northern charity into a globally balanced partner of choice for activists around the world. This is not only a good thing, it's essential if Oxfam wants to speak the language of emerging global activism. In my experience, younger activists, steeped in postmodernist identity and values, have little time for those who fail to examine their own roots, identity, privilege or prejudices.

This work is not easy. Donors, supporters, partners and movements don't engage inequality activists so that we can make *ourselves* better. They want us fighting against inequality *for others*. We are reaching a critical moment for inequality activism. Change is coming to our world. The struggle will be over the *kind* of change that comes. For activists who do the "inner work" of self-examination, we can shape that change both by who we are and what we fight for. We can, for example, aim to be feminist and anti-racist not just in our own lives; but we can work towards *A Feminist Future* (September, 2020) that cares for social justice, the planet and the 99% of humanity who deserve a better deal.[10]

For American activists to help reset economic rules, we must find power across our intersecting and diverging identities, economic, political and demographic. To do that, we must challenge each other on our own power. Hopefully, if we keep the end in mind, we can be part of a much bigger power switch that reverses extreme inequalities for good.

References and Notes

Books

Alexander, Michelle, *The New Jim Crow: Mass Incarceration in the Age of Color Blindness* The New Press (2010)

Easterly, Bill, *The White Man's Burden: Why the West's Efforts to Aid the Rest have Done So Much Ill and So Little Good* (2007)

Foucault, Michael, *Words and Things* (1966)

Foucault, Michael, *Discipline and Punish* (1975)

Foucault, Michael, *The History of Sexuality* (1976) Éditions Gallimard

Friedman, Milton, *Capitalism and Freedom:* Fortieth Anniversary Edition, University of Chicago Press (2002)

Giridharadas, Anand, *Winners Take All, The Elite Charade of Changing the World* (2019)

Hartwick, Elaine, *Theories of Development* (Third Edition, 2015)

Heimans, Jeremy and Timms, Henry, *New Power, How Power Works in Our Hyperconnected World — and How to Make It Work for You* (2018)

Hobbes, Thomas, *Leviathan* (1651) Penguin Classics

Lukes, Steven, *Power: A Radical View* (second Ed. 2005). (First edition in 1973)

Mitchell, George E, Schmitz, Hans Peter, & Bruno van-Vijfeijken, Tosca, *Between Power and Irrelevance: The Future of Transnational NGOs* (July 2020)

Moyo, Dambisa, *Dead Aid* (2009)

Nietzsche, Frederich, *Thus Spoke Zarathustra* (1883) and *Beyond Good and Evil* (1887)

Phillips, Ben, *How to Fight Inequality: And Why That Fight Needs You* (September, 2020)

Sandel, Michael, *What Money Can't Buy: The Moral Limits of Markets* (2012)

Weber, Max, *Politics as a Vocation, in* The Vocation Essays (1919)

Zucman, Gabriel, *The Hidden Wealth of Nations* (2015)

Videos, Films and Podcasts

How to Survive a Plague, The Inside Story of How Citizens and Activists Tamed AIDS, (2012)[1]

Naomi Klein, *Coronavirus Capitalism — And How to Beat It*[2]

Chinese Government Video on How to Fight Coronavirus with a new Social Compact[3]

Nadia Daar, Max Lawson, Nabil Ahmed, *Equals*, The Inequality Podcast[4] (2020 ongoing)

Ben Rhodes, *Missing America,* Podcast5 (2020 ongoing)

Oxfam Reports and Media Briefs Referenced in this Book

Working for the Few: Political Capture and Economic Inequality (2014)[1]

Public Good or Private Wealth (January 2019)[2]

Time to Care: Unpaid and Underpaid Care Work and the Global Inequality Crisis (January 2020)[3]

Dignity not Destitution: An 'Economic Rescue Plan for All' to tackle the Coronavirus crisis and Rebuild a More Equal World (March 2020)[4]

Conflict in the Time of Coronavirus (May 2020)[5]

Caring Under COVID-19: How the Pandemic Is – and Is Not – Changing Unpaid Care and Domestic Work Responsibilities in the U.S. (June 2020) (With Promundo)[6]

¿Quien Paga la cuenta? Who Pays the bill? Taxing Wealth to face the COVID-19 Crisis in Latin America and the Caribbean (July 2020)[7]

The Hunger Virus: How COVID-19 is Fueling Hunger in a Hungry World (July 2020)[8]

For a Decade of Hope Not Austerity in The Middle East and North Africa (August 2020)[9]

Power, Profits and the Pandemic (September 2020)[10]

Feminist Futures: Caring for People, Caring for Justice and Rights (September 2020)[11]

End Notes

Videos, Films and Podcasts

1 https://surviveaplague.com/
2 https://theintercept.com/2020/03/16/coronavirus-capitalism/
3 https://m.facebook.com/story.php?story_fbid=10157056790413354&id=617278353
4 https://www.buzzsprout.com/606307
5 https://crooked.com/podcast-series/missing-america/

Oxfam Reports

1 https://www-cdn.oxfam.org/s3fs-public/file_attachments/bp-working-for-few-political-capture-economic-inequality-200114-en_3.pdf
2 https://www.oxfam.org/en/research/working-few
3 https://www.oxfam.org/en/research/time-care
4 https://www.oxfam.org/en/research/dignity-not-destitution
5 https://www.oxfam.org/en/research/conflict-time-coronavirus
6 https://men-care.org/resources/caring-under-COVID-19-how-the-pandemic-is-and-is-not-changing-unpaid-care-and-domestic-work-responsibilities/
7 https://www.oxfam.org/es/informes/quien-paga-la-cuenta-gravar-la-riqueza-para-enfrentar-la-crisis-de-la-COVID-19-en-america
8 https://www.oxfam.org/en/research/hunger-virus-how-COVID-19-fuelling-hunger-hungry-world
9 https://www.oxfam.org/en/press-releases/mena-billionaires-wealth-increased-10-billion-enough-pay-beirut-blast-repair-bill
10 https://www.oxfam.org/en/research/power-profits-and-

pandemic

11 https://oxfamilibrary.openrepository.com/
handle/10546/621046

Prologue: A Possible Future

1 "Inequality virus" is a phrase I first heard and read from
my Oxfam colleague Nabil Ahmed. Read his remarkable
blog which explains it here.

https://www.weforum.org/agenda/2020/07/covid19-
inequality-billionaires-oxfam/

Chapter 1. International Activism: A Field in Flux

1 That is, until they get asked tougher questions "Who have
you helped and how deeply?" Or "Tell us about the people,
communities or countries that are now resilient to a shock
like this pandemic." Then the data often arrives on people
helped directly or through partners.

2 Donnelly, E, *Proclaiming the Jubilee, the Debt and Structural
Adjustment Network*, Available at https://www.worldhunger.
org/articles/hn/debtcrisisnet.pdf at 3

3 Roodman, David *The Arc of the Jubilee,* October 2010, Essay,
Center for Global Development https://www.cgdev.org/
sites/default/files/1424539_file_Roodman_Jubilee_FINAL.
pdf

4 Soskis, Benjamin, *The Founding of the Center for Global
Development,* Open Philanthropy Project History Case
Study.   https://www.openphilanthropy.org/files/History_
of_Philanthropy/CGD/Case_Study_CGD_Founding.pdf
I've heard Ed Scott tell this same story at the retirement of
one of CGD's co-founders, Nancy Birdsall in 2016.

5 https://en.wikipedia.org/wiki/Make_Poverty_
History#:~:text=The%20Make%20Poverty%20History%20
campaign,into%20taking%20actions%20towards%20
relieving

6   Currion, Paul *Decolonising Aid, Again,* July 2020, The New Humanitarian. https://www.thenewhumanitarian.org/opinion/2020/07/13/decolonisation-aid-humanitarian-development-racism-black-lives-matter

7   Kripke, Gawain *The Makings of Feminist Foreign Aid,* July 31, 2017, The Politics of Poverty, https://politicsofpoverty.oxfamamerica.org/the-makings-of-feminist-foreign-aid/

Chapter 2: A Strange Thing about Power and Money

1   That said, he always "presupposes that power is a kind of power-over" https://plato.stanford.edu/entries/feminist-power/#DefPow and he puts it "if we speak of the structures or the mechanisms of power, it is only insofar as we suppose that certain persons exercise power over others." *Afterword: The Subject and Power* in Hubert Dreyfus and Paul Rabinow, Michel Foucault: Beyond Structuralism and Hermeneutics, 2nd edition. Chicago: University of Chicago Press (1983).

2   The best overview I've found of feminist theory on development is by Elaine Hartwick in *Theories of Development* (Third Edition, 2015). See Chapter Seven which interrogates five strands of feminist theory (Women in Development, Women and Development, Gender and Development, Women, Environment and Development and Postmodernism and Development).

3   Writing in 1984, the year of Foucault's death, Chandra Mohanty used Foucault's work on power to deconstruct how Western white-led voices were beginning to assert their own colonial hegemony over feminist approaches to "humanism"—the forebearer of the SDGs. She was one of the early thinkers exploring how Southern women of color were defined as "Others" or peripheral to these debates. Chandra Mohanty, Vol. 12, No. 3, *On Humanism and the University I: The Discourse of Humanism.* (spring–autumn, 1984), pp. 333–358.

4 One of the most interesting groups thinking about power and racial justice in the United States is Change Elemental, whose tag line demonstrates that they have taken power debates beyond zero-sum thinking: "Co-creating Power for Love, Dignity and Justice." See www.changeelemental.org.

5 One of the most influential for the development community is John Gaventa whose work *Power and Powerlessness: Quiescence and Rebellion in an Appalachian Valley*, (1980) applied Luke's three dimensions to examine why those on the wrong end of economic and political power equations do not rise in rebellion.

6 Reproductive rights groups have been at the forefront of challenging attempts by States to assert power over the sexual health and reproductive rights of women. One of the groups leading those efforts in the United States, see the Center for Health and Gender Equity www.genderhealth.org., and www.plannedparenthood.com.

7 Jeremy Heimans and Henry Timms wrote a fascinating book called *New Power: How Power Works In our Hyper Connected World—and How to Make It Work for You* (2018). I would argue, however, that it is less the "power" that's new in their book, than the ways in which power moves through the world—less like a currency held by a few elites, and more like a current that is "open, participatory and peer driven."

8 In a chapter of another book, I go into those philosophical debates. "Left Behind or Pushed Behind? Redistributing Power Over the Sustainable Development Goals", in *Leave No One Behind* (2019). https://www.brookings.edu/wp-content/uploads/2019/09/LNOB_Chapter13.pdf.

9 Zoltan Grossman, *Remember the 80s* https://www.counterpunch.org/2008/01/03/remember-the-80s/. The best resource I've found on the success of Act Up, is here www.surviveaplague.com. The movie is one of the best how-to

guides to effective campaigning I know.

10 O'Brien Paul, *"Left Behind or Pushed Behind? Redistributing Power Over the Sustainable Development Goals"*, https://www.brookings.edu/wp-content/uploads/2019/09/LNOB_Chapter13.pdf. In *Leave No One Behind, Time for Specifics on the Sustainable Development Goals*, Ed. Brookings (2019)

11 https://en.wikipedia.org/wiki/Gross_world_product

Chapter 3: When Power Switches Happen

1 Freedman, Milton, *Capitalism and Freedom* (1982 Preface) fortieth Anniversary Edition at xiv.

2 Renshon, Stanley A. *Barack Obama and the Politics of Redemption* (2012).

3 Benjamin Page et al., *Democracy and the Policy Preferences of Wealthy Americans* https://faculty.wcas.northwestern.edu/~jnd260/cab/CAB2012%20-%20Page1.pdf

4 Krugman, Paul, *Why Do the Rich Have So Much Power*, July 1 2020 https://www.nytimes.com/2020/07/01/opinion/sunday/inequality-america-paul-krugman.html?action=click&module=Opinion&pgtype=Homepage

5 Tracking coronavirus global spread https://www.cnn.com/interactive/2020/health/coronavirus-maps-and-cases/. Accessed on Sep 28, 2020

6 India's Economy Shrinks by a Quarter as covid-19 gathers pace, Sep 3, 2020, https://www.economist.com/asia/2020/09/03/indias-economy-shrinks-by-a-quarter-as-covid-19-gathers-pace

7 Solis, Maria, *Coronavirus is the Perfect Disaster for "Disaster Capitalism"* https://www.vice.com/en_us/article/5dmqyk/naomi-klein-interview-on-coronavirus-and-disaster-capitalism-shock-doctrine

8 Torry, Harriet, *U.S. Economy Contracted at Record Rate Last Quarter; Jobless Claims Rise to 1.43 Million*, July 30, 2020 https://www.wsj.com/articles/us-economy-gdp-report-

second-quarter-coronavirus-11596061406

9   The Economist, *A Rift in Democratic Attitudes Is Opening Up Around the World,* Accessed August 22, 2020. https://www.economist.com/graphic-detail/2020/08/22/a-rift-in-democratic-attitudes-is-opening-up-around-the-world

Chapter 4: From an Inequality Virus to Coronavirus

1   Ronald Reagan, *Inaugural Address,* January 20, 1981, https://www.reaganfoundation.org/ronald-reagan/reagan-quotes-speeches/inaugural-address-2/

2   See e.g. Alexander, Michelle, *The New Jim Crow: Mass Incarceration in the Age of Color Blindness* (2010) The New Press

3   Oxfam, *Public Good or Private Wealth, Methodology Note* (January 2019). https://indepth.oxfam.org.uk/public-good-private-wealth/

4   Oxfam, *Public Good or Private Wealth, Methodology Note* (January 2019)
     https://indepth.oxfam.org.uk/public-good-private-wealth/

5   Oxfam *Power, Profits and the Pandemic* 2020 at 12. Data obtained by Oxfam from https://fortune.com/global500/; 2009 data obtained from: https://money.cnn.com/magazines/fortune/global500/2009/full_list/index.html.

6   Oxfam *Power, Profits and the Pandemic* (Sept 2020) at 13.

7   Oxfam *Power, Profits and the Pandemic* (Sept 2020) at 13. Oxfam analysis based on company earnings statements; Capital IQ.

8   Shaxson, Nicholas, *Tackling Tax Havens*, (Sep 2019) https://www.imf.org/external/pubs/ft/fandd/2019/09/tackling-global-tax-havens-shaxon.htm   -   :~:text=Individuals%20have%20stashed%20%248.7%20trillion,of%20up%20to%20%2436%20trillion.

9   Zucman Gabriel *The Hidden Wealth of Nations* (2015)

10   *Bill Gates Timeline* Forbes (2006) https://www.forbes.

com/2006/06/16/cz_rr_ck_billgatesslide.html - 374438183811

11 Berger, *Sarah Jeff Bezos Gave Away More Money than Bill Gates, Mark Zuckerberg Combined in 2018,* (Feb 13, 2020) https://www.cnbc.com/2019/02/13/philanthropy-50-how-much-bezos-gates-zuckerberg-charities-gave-away.html

12 https://www.forbes.com/profile/bill-gates/ (Accessed Sept 16 2020)

13 Oxfam, *Power Profits and the Pandemic* (Sept 2020) at 24.

14 Oxfam, *Public Good or Private Wealth, Methodology Note* (January 2019) at 18

15 Tankersley, Jim, *Why Trump's Approval Ratings On the Economy Remain Durable* (Aug 24, 2020) (https://www.nytimes.com/2020/08/24/us/politics/trump-economy.html

16 https://www.aljazeera.com/news/2018/12/protests-rising-prices-spread-sudan-khartoum-181220132130661.html

17 https://politicsofpoverty.oxfamamerica.org/2019/11/protests-chile-inequality-social-justice/

18 https://www.pri.org/stories/2019-10-24/how-lebanons-whatsapp-tax-unleashed-flood-anger

19 https://www.npr.org/2018/12/03/672862353/who-are-frances-yellow-vest-protesters-and-what-do-they-want

20 https://www.miamiherald.com/news/nation-world/world/americas/haiti/article214490259.html

21 https://www.washingtonpost.com/world/the_americas/ecuadors-indigenous-people-are-leading-the-nations-anti-government-protests-they-have-a-record-of-ousting-presidents/2019/10/10/ab9d7f1e-eaa2-11e9-a329-7378fbfa1b63_story.html

22 https://www.economist.com/middle-east-and-africa/2019/11/21/rises-in-the-price-of-petrol-are-fuelling-unrest-in-iran

23 https://www.hrw.org/world-report/2019/country-chapters/guinea

24 https://www.nytimes.com/2019/11/20/world/middleeast/

iraq-protests-sadr-city.html

25 https://www.aljazeera.com/news/2019/11/students-india-delhi-launch-fee-protests-191123111932787.html

26 https://www.weforum.org/agenda/2016/01/inequality-is-getting-worse-in-latin-america-here-s-how-to-fix-it/

27 https://www.nytimes.com/2019/11/08/opinion/contributors/latin-america-protest-repression.html

28 https://foreignpolicy.com/2020/07/06/global-poverty-rampant-un-misleading/

29 https://www.nytimes.com/interactive/2020/07/02/opinion/politics/us-economic-social-inequality.html?action=click&module=Opinion&pgtype=Homepage

30 https://www.socialprogress.org/?tab=2&code=USA

31 https://www.nytimes.com/2020/09/09/opinion/united-states-social-progress.html

32 https://www.nytimes.com/interactive/2020/07/02/opinion/politics/us-economic-social-inequality.html?action=click&module=Opinion&pgtype=Homepage

33 https://www.oxfamireland.org/blog/women-bearing-burden-fight-against-coronavirus

34 Oxfam America and Promundo, *Caring Under COVID-19: How the Pandemic Is – and Is Not – Changing Unpaid Care and Domestic Work Responsibilities in the U.S.*, https://men-care.org/resources/caring-under-COVID-19-how-the-pandemic-is-and-is-not-changing-unpaid-care-and-domestic-work-responsibilities/

35 https://twitter.com/ONS/status/1271367085302730753?ref_src=twsrc%5Etfw%7Ctwcamp%5Etweetembed%7Ctwterm%5E1271367085302730753%7Ctwgr%5E&ref_url=https%3A%2F%2Fwww.huffingtonpost.co.uk%2Fentry%2Fcoronavirus-mortality-rate-ons-england_uk_5ee34d76c5b63db52533e413

36 https://www.worldometers.info/coronavirus/coronavirus-death-toll/

37 https://www.oxfamamerica.org/explore/stories/12000-people-could-die-each-day-hunger-linked-covid-19/

38 https://www.wfp.org/news/world-food-programme-assist-largest-number-hungry-people-ever-coronavirus-devastates-poor

39 Oxfam, *Power, Profits and the Pandemic* (September 2020), at 21

40 Id at 26

41 Id at 28

42 https://www.oxfam.org/en/press-releases/latin-american-billionaires-surge-worlds-most-unequal-region-buckles

43 https://www.oxfam.org/en/press-releases/latin-american-billionaires-surge-worlds-most-unequal-region-buckles

Chapter 5: Strategic Challenges for U.S. Activists

1 https://obamawhitehouse.archives.gov/the-press-office/2017/01/18/remarks-vice-president-joe-biden-world-economic-forum

2 https://carnegieendowment.org/2020/09/09/new-u.s.-foreign-policy-for-post-pandemic-landscape-pub-82498

3 https://en.wikipedia.org/wiki/The_Squad_(United_States_Congress)

4 https://crooked.com/podcast-series/missing-america/

5 Ben Rhodes, *The World as It Is: A Memoir of the Obama White House* at 45

6 https://thedailyrecord.com/2012/01/31/bidens-american-exceptionalism-and-the-rule-of-law/

7 https://www.pewresearch.org/fact-tank/2017/06/30/most-americans-say-the-u-s-is-among-the-greatest-countries-in-the-world/

8 https://www.irishtimes.com/opinion/fintan-o-toole-donald-trump-has-destroyed-the-country-he-promised-to-make-great-again-1.4235928

9 https://www.nytimes.com/live/2020/07/23/business/stock-

market-today-coronavirus

10 https://www.fcnl.org/updates/building-the-movement-for-a-new-peaceful-foreign-policy-2465

11 https://www.commondreams.org/views/2019/04/18/jimmy-carter-us-most-warlike-nation-history-world

12 https://www.nytimes.com/2020/09/08/magazine/displaced-war-on-terror.html?searchResultPosition=1

13 https://www.economist.com/international/2020/08/11/how-much-does-americas-missing-diplomatic-leadership-matter

14 https://www.brookings.edu/blog/africa-in-focus/2019/07/10/figure-of-the-week-chinas-hidden-lending-in-africa/

15 https://www.usaidalumni.org/uaa-forum/forum-1/agency-notice-from-the-administrator-usaids-response-to-great-power-competition-the-clear-choice-framework/

16 Yuen Yuen Ang, *Demystifying Belt and Road: The Struggle to Define China's Project of the Century* Foreign Affairs (May 22, 2019 https://www.foreignaffairs.com/articles/china/2019-05-22/demystifying-belt-and-road

17 https://m.facebook.com/story.php?story_fbid=10157056790413354&id=617278353

18 https://www.cfr.org/backgrounder/chinas-repression-uighurs-xinjiang

19 https://www.theatlantic.com/ideas/archive/2020/07/pompeos-surreal-speech-on-china/614596/

20 https://www.washingtonpost.com/news/wonk/wp/2015/03/24/how-china-used-more-cement-in-3-years-than-the-u-s-did-in-the-entire-20th-century/

21 https://www.washingtonpost.com/graphics/2020/politics/reckoning-america-world-standing-low-point/

22 https://www.state.gov/communist-china-and-the-free-worlds-future/

23 https://www.nytimes.com/interactive/2020/science/

coronavirus-vaccine-tracker.html#sinovac

24 Elizabeth Ralph, *What Happens if China Gets the COVID-19 Vaccine First?* https://www.politico.com/news/magazine/2020/08/31/china-covid-19-vaccine-first-401636

25 *Vaccine Rationing and the Urgency of Social Justice in the COVID-19 response,* https://onlinelibrary.wiley.com/doi/10.1002/hast.1113

26 Emmanuel, Ezekiel et al, *An Ethical Framework for Global Vaccine Allocation,* September 2020. https://science.sciencemag.org/content/early/2020/09/02/science.abe2803#:~:text=The%20Fair%20Priority%20Model%20specifies,efforts%20at%20a%20fair%20distribution.

27 https://home.kpmg/xx/en/home/insights/2020/04/international-monetary-fund-government-and-institution-measures-in-response-to-covid.html

28 https://www.unhcr.org/en-us/figures-at-a-glance.html

29 https://g20.org/en/media/Documents/G20_Extraordinary%20G20%20Leaders%E2%80%99%20Summit_Statement_EN%20(3).pdf

30 https://www.washingtonpost.com/graphics/2020/politics/reckoning-america-world-standing-low-point/

31 https://news.gallup.com/poll/116350/position-world.aspx

32 https://carnegieendowment.org/2020/09/09/new-u.s.-foreign-policy-for-post-pandemic-landscape-pub-82498

33 https://www.cnn.com/2019/10/09/world/gallery/extinction-rebellion-intl-gbr/index.html

34 https://www.usatoday.com/story/news/politics/2020/07/18/rep-john-lewis-most-memorable-quotes-get-good-trouble/5464148002/

35 https://www.un.org/sg/en/content/sg/statement/2020-09-01/secretary-generals-remarks-virtual-high-level-meeting-generation-unlimited-%E2%80%9Cconnecting-half-the-world-opportunities-delivered

Chapter 6: To Switch Power, Follow the Money

1 https://www-cdn.oxfam.org/s3fs-public/file_attachments/bp-working-for-few-political-capture-economic-inequality-200114-en_3.pdf

2 In *The Haves and Have Nots* (2011), Branko Milanovich argued that three forms of economic inequality matter: between individuals in a nation, between countries in the world, and between all citizens across the world. All three forms of inequality are growing in this pandemic, but for international activists, the latter two are most worrying.

3 https://www.oxfam.org/en/research/dignity-not-destitution

4 https://www.economist.com/middle-east-and-africa/2020/06/06/african-governments-face-a-wall-of-debt-repayments

5 https://www.voanews.com/east-asia-pacific/voa-news-china/china-worlds-biggest-creditor-delays-debt-repayments-77-nations#:~:text=China%20is%20currently%20the%20largest,obligations%20were%20owed%20to%20China

6 Thomas Torslov, Ludvig S. Wier, Gabriel Zucman, *The Missing Profits of Nations.* https://www.nber.org/papers/w24701

7 https://www.imf.org/external/pubs/ft/wp/2015/wp15118.pdf

8 Gabriel Zucman, *The Hidden Wealth of Nations* (2015). https://www.econ.berkeley.edu/content/hidden-wealth-nations-scourge-tax-havens

9 ICRICT Report: *The Global Pandemic, Sustainable Economic Recovery and International Taxation* (June 2020) https://static1.squarespace.com/static/5a0c602bf43b5594845abb81/t/5ee6dab18a33630b03bcf2e1/1592187569589/Exec+summary+%26+key+stats_+EMBARGOED+15+June+9h00+EDT.pdf

10 See *Oxfam's Media Brief with our 5-point plan, Endless Corporate*

Tax Scandals? https://oxfamilibrary.openrepository.com/bitstream/handle/10546/620848/mb-endless-corporate-tax-scandals-mauritius-290719-en.pdf

11 An interactive map of 30 countries where Oxfam has worked on extractive industries can be found at http://eimap.oxfam.org/

12 https://www.icrict.com/press-release/2020/6/14/icrict-report-the-global-pandemic-sustainable-economic-recovery-and-international-taxation

13 These recommendations are drawn largely from Oxfam's 5-point plan and the ICRICT Report (June 2020) cited above.

14 https://www.cgdev.org/blog/how-g20-finance-ministers-can-act-responsibly-sdr-reallocation

15 https://www.theguardian.com/global-development/2015/jul/06/make-poverty-history-campaign-gleneagles-sustainable-development-goals

16 I heard this first from the Editor in Chief of Devex, Raj Kumar.

17 Elizabeth Ralph, *What Happens if China Gets the COVID-19 Vaccine First?* https://www.politico.com/news/magazine/2020/08/31/china-COVID-19-vaccine-first-401636

18 https://www.politico.com/news/magazine/2020/08/31/china-COVID-19-vaccine-first-401636

19 https://www.rollingstone.com/politics/political-commentary/COVID-19-end-of-american-era-wade-davis-1038206/

20 Oxfam, *The Hunger Virus* (July 2020) at 1

21 https://www.nytimes.com/2020/09/11/business/covid-hunger-food-insecurity.html

22 Oxfam, *The Hunger Virus* (July 2020) at 1–5

Conclusion

1 https://en.wikipedia.org/wiki/Overton_window#:~:text=The%20Overton%20window%20is%20

the,is%20named%20after%20Joseph%20P

2   *How to Fight Inequality* (2020) at 53

3   https://www.oxfamamerica.org/press/more-two-dozen-groups-ensure-presidential-candidates-discuss-international-issues-us-world-makes-foreign-affairs-part-2020-debate/

4   While campaigning in Indiana, Joe Biden promised an interview with the initiative, but his people eventually backed him out of it. Either they felt confident that progressive internationalists would show up for Biden regardless, didn't want him on the record on our issues, or didn't need him in the spotlight while Trump was self-destructing in early 2020

5   *Rich Countries Call Dibs on Covid-19 vaccines,* https://www.oxfamamerica.org/explore/stories/rich-countries-call-dibs-covid-19-vaccines-image/

6   *Power Profits and the Pandemic*

7   https://sur.conectas.org/en/oxfams-behind-brands-code-corporate-campaigning/

8   https://www.oxfamamerica.org/explore/research-publications/the-commitment-to-reducing-inequality-index-2020/

9   https://www.bbc.com/news/uk-43112200?intlink_from_url=&link_location=live-reporting-story

10 https://oxfamilibrary.openrepository.com/handle/10546/621046

CHANGEMAKERS
BOOKS

TRANSFORMATION

Transform your life, transform your world – Changemakers Books publishes for individuals committed to transforming their lives and transforming the world. Our readers seek to become
positive, powerful agents of change. Changemakers Books inform, inspire, and provide practical wisdom and skills to empower us to write the next chapter of humanity's future.
www.changemakers-books.com

The *Resilience* Series

The Resilience Series is a collaborative effort by the authors of Changemakers Books in response to the 2020 coronavirus epidemic. Each concise volume offers expert advice and practical exercises for mastering specific skills and abilities. Our intention is that by strengthening your resilience, you can better survive and even thrive in a time of crisis.
www.resilience-books.com

Adapt and Plan for the New Abnormal – in the COVID-19 Coronavirus Pandemic
Gleb Tsipursky

Aging with Vision, Hope and Courage in a Time of Crisis
John C. Robinson

Connecting with Nature in a Time of Crisis
Melanie Choukas-Bradley

Going Within in a Time of Crisis
P. T. Mistlberger

Grow Stronger in a Time of Crisis
Linda Ferguson

Handling Anxiety in a Time of Crisis
George Hoffman

Navigating Loss in a Time of Crisis
Jules De Vitto

The Life-Saving Skill of Story
Michelle Auerbach

Virtual Teams – Holding the Center When You Can't Meet Face-to-Face
Carlos Valdes-Dapena

Virtually Speaking – Communicating at a Distance
Tim Ward and Teresa Erickson

Current Bestsellers from Changemakers Books

Pro Truth
A Practical Plan for Putting Truth Back into Politics
Gleb Tsipursky and Tim Ward

How can we turn back the tide of post-truth politics, fake news, and misinformation that is damaging our democracy? In the lead up to the 2020 US Presidential Election, Pro Truth provides the answers.

An Antidote to Violence
Evaluating the Evidence
Barry Spivack and Patricia Anne Saunders

It's widely accepted that Transcendental Meditation can create peace for the individual, but can it create peace in society as a whole? And if it can, what could possibly be the mechanism?

Finding Solace at Theodore Roosevelt Island
Melanie Choukas-Bradley

A woman seeks solace on an urban island paradise in Washington D.C. through 2016–17, and the shock of the Trump election.

the bottom
a theopoetic of the streets
Charles Lattimore Howard

An exploration of homelessness fusing theology, jazz-verse and intimate storytelling into a challenging, raw and beautiful tale.

The Soul of Activism
A Spirituality for Social Change
Shmuly Yanklowitz

A unique examination of the power of interfaith spirituality to fuel the fires of progressive activism.

Future Consciousness
The Path to Purposeful Evolution
Thomas Lombardo

An empowering evolutionary vision of wisdom and the human mind to guide us in creating a positive future.

Preparing for a World that Doesn't Exist – Yet
Rick Smyre and Neil Richardson

This book is about an emerging Second Enlightenment and the capacities you will need to achieve success in this new, fast-evolving world.